ORGANIZE AND SIMPLIFY YOUR LIFE

---

*Effective Strategies to Make Time for
What Matters Most to You*

John Williams

TABLE OF CONTENTS

Introduction

Are you harboring things that were never meant to grow in your life? It is time to stop it. Understand what is good for you, what works for you, and what is right for you. Even though we want to change some things about yourself, you cannot fix all of them. Some things were to remain the way they are.

You are nearing your season of greatness by making the right choices. Making the right choices no matter how hard they may seem to be will make you harvest what you have never seen before.

The road to greatness in life is without challenges, disappointments, and failures. This, however, should not be a stumbling block to achieving your goals. Overcoming them is simple—you have to make a few adjustments that will suit you. Never settle for the clouds when aiming the stars.

What Is Life All About?

Did you know that simplifying and organizing our life will help you live better? Life often loses meaning when one fails to find its meaning and significance. Learning ways of organizing and simplifying your life can change your perspective of life. Some of the important factors that can make life difficult without good management include time, finance, eating methods, etc. If not managed well, this life could seem like hell on earth.

Through organizing and simplifying your life, you will live happier, and you will be in control of your life better. You will be able to anticipate future happenings with certainty. Sometimes you feel too weighed down when trying to make too many things work your way. This should not be the case. You are not a machine—be realistic to your abilities.

It will take a little of your energy to create a discipline working formula for your life. Relieve the stress and bring back joy to your life through simple efforts. Some called it meditation or taking time for yourself. This makes you understand who you really are and what you want in life.

Things You Can Never Change in Your Life

Did you know that you can never change your life just by working hard? The secret to a successful life is found on the simple things you do on a daily basis. There are, however, things you can never change in your life. Here are five truths about your life:

1. **You are accountable for your actions**. Sometimes you are tempted to stretch your moral boundaries or take a shortcut to achieve some outcome. It is, therefore, important to realize that any action has a reaction. Be ready to take responsibility for whatever action you take.

2. **You will not live forever.** Life is too short not to take good care of it. In an effort to achieve your goals, you are forced to push yourself too hard. This circumstances often force you to miss your vacation or important activities such as workouts.

3. **You can never get back to yesterday.** You can never change your past. However much you regret about your past, the best thing to do is accept your mistakes, learn from them, and move on.

4. **The world cannot change for you.** Be flexible to the changing world. It is important to note, however, that it is your duty to change the world. Some things are too big for us to change. If your efforts of changing some things in the world do not go as expected, at least you tried. Do not go knocking your head on the wall.

5. **You cannot change where you came from.** No one in the world chose the race, country, or tribe you are born to. While others are privileged to be born in wealthy families, others have to work hard to live a good life. Do not use your background as an excuse for your failures. Achieve your goals wherever you are.

Chapter 1

Organize and Simplify Your Life

Are you content with the way your life is going? Have you been doing the same thing over the years and getting the same results? Are you yearning to live a meaningful life but don't know how to achieve it?

The answer to those questions is in organizing and simplifying your life. The choice of improving your life by organizing and simplifying is not a destination but rather a journey. What works for me may not necessarily work for you since we are all different.

Things that bring joy to you could be a source of sorrow to me. The essential thing is to realize the things that spark joy in your life and find a way of using them to improve your life.

The Importance of Simplifying and Organizing Your Life

Although it is every person's dream to live a good and happy life, people struggle with sustaining their emotions, their mindset, and even their lifestyle. In addition, you get too many nuggets of advice, some contradicting each other. This problem is common not only to you but also to so many people. Here are the reasons why it is important to take control of your life.

1. **Your mind will be cleared.** Did you know that by putting up a plan on what you have to do in order to succeed helps you feel renewed? Although you have not actually done the job, your stress levels will largely be reduced. Actually having a game

plan on what you are about to do helps you feel like your problem is actually solved already.

2. **It saves you money and time.** Did you know that people spend half of their income on buying what they had not planned for? Yes, impulsive buying is consuming most of your funds. Stop living on guesswork and start understanding what you want and when you want it. Many times, you are left brainstorming on what you have been eating the whole week in an effort to decide what you will cook today. You are wasting your time. Have a dinner timetable. It will actually save a lot of your time. In addition, you will be able to live a healthy lifestyle.

3. **It allows for flexibility.** Yes, you will have extra time to do unscheduled situations. Organizing and simplifying your life does not mean leaving your social life or friends. On the contrary, it will help you socialize more. The only difference is that you are under control of every situation. There is a negative perception out there that having a game plan in your life actually denies you from having fun. Try it. You will have more time to have fun.

4. **It makes you a good role model.** Did you know that your kids follow your footsteps in everything you do? To them, the lifestyle they see you living is the right one. The food you eat, how you manage your time, how you spend your money, and everything you do are important. Be a good example. You will not want to knock your head down in the future, cursing yourself for not being a good role model for your kids.

5. **It is actually contagious.** It is true! Living a simple and organized life can spread like fire on a bush. My relatives, neighbors, and colleagues at work have praised my way of life. Yes, they even come to me for advice, many jumping into my boat. Take the same journey as me and realize the number of people you will change.

6. **Boost your self-esteem.** The best thing for every person is the feeling of accomplishment. Eating healthy every day, paying your bills on time, having time for your family, and finishing your day's work on time—these are the things that make life beautiful. The feeling of doing the right thing at the right time boosts your self-esteem. You will always feel proud of your efforts. Start living a simple and organized life and realize the sweetness of life!

7. **You will love your home.** Doing your chores on time, putting things where there are supposed to be, and disposing of what you don't need—these simple things will allow you to identify the areas you need to improve in your home. At times, people complain of their house being too small. This may not be the case. Dispose of what you do not need to make room for things you need.

8. **It improves your family relations.** This is actually the most important of all. With a flexible time schedule, your family is aware of all your moves. This avoids the stress of asking too many questions of your whereabouts every time you are not home.

Your family will follow you, and they will adopt your habits. In the long run, you will all be on the same page. It will help you spend less time on things that are not important and focus on things that matter.

Methods of Organizing and Strategizing Your Life

Unlike in the past, the dynamics of life have greatly changed. The economic situations, the increasing pressure of the depleted resources, and many others have contributed to the difficulties of life. It's time to swallow your pride and start looking for the best methods of organizing your life.

I have seen people argue that being organized in life is an inborn trait. I will, however, differ with such arguments; I believe that it is a choice for everyone to make. It is a matter of putting things together, knowing what you want your life to be, ditching the unnecessary practices, and being disciplined to yourself.

If you are thinking ways to turn your life around by strategizing and organizing, this is the book for you! Take that bold step of putting your life together. It is simple to follow the following steps and put a smile on your face every day.

1. Put Everything into Writing

It is not a secret that it is tough to keep everything in your memory. Instead of stopping every time to think of what to do next, how would it be if you were just to refer your notes? It will not only save your time but also serve as a reminder.

Create an external brain through pen and paper or a digital brain through your iPad or your computer. Trying to keep all your schedules in your brain will complicate your life more instead of making it better.

Events such as birthdays, deadlines, and meetings should be indicated somewhere. Can you imagine skipping your child's or girlfriend/boyfriend's birthday? Writing down these dates will help you in budgeting, hence making your life better.

2. Keep Everything in Their Place

How much time do you waste looking for those little things that you misplace in your house or office? Be it a knife in your kitchen, a pen in your office, or a wheel spanner in your car. Stop this hustle by creating a suitable place for all your items.

Making your life organized means keeping everything in its place. How organized is your home? How do you keep your thing? Do you label things on where they are supposed to be? This is the questions you must ask yourself to realize whether you are doing things right.

Since you are not in your house every time, let those you share a house or workplace know where you keep your things. Creativity is key when it comes to finding the most suitable places for various items. When you find it difficult to choose the most suitable place, try experimenting. Trust me, eventually, you will find the most suitable places for your items.

In the past, I used to have a problem with pens in my office. I used to buy a pen more than three times each week. Trust me, the last time I bought a set of pens was three months ago, and it seems like I am not buying them anytime soon. Look at the cost I have saved by purchasing a simple item.

3. Learn to Delegate Your Duties

You are not a superman! As much as you want to accomplish everything that is on your to-do list, do whatever you can and delegate responsibilities elsewhere. Note that delegating your duties elsewhere is not a sign of laziness but a strength. The most important thing is ensuring that everything goes as planned.

After waking up in the morning, go through your to-do list and indicate your duties for the day. It is also important to vet the people whom you will delegate your duties. Ensure that you trust them with your work. If you randomly assign your duties, be ready to be disappointed.

It is important that you get in touch with a person you assigned the job. In case the person has any challenges, step in and help. Letting the person finish the job without communication may result in a misunderstanding if the job is not done well.

4. Stop Procrastinating

To ensure a less stressful life, take the step to organize and strategize your life. The longer you wait to take that step, the more complicated things continue to be. Did you know that an effort you put today relieves the pressure you are to go through tomorrow?

Whatever you do today will never be equivalent to tomorrow's work. Tomorrow is another day different from today. Make use of today as if it were the end of the world. Postpone only things that you are forced by circumstances and cannot do them.

5. Always Ensure That You Are Tidy

Cleaning up is one of the most important factors that contribute a lot in your life. The mind works best under a clean and well-varnished environment. Also, to live a healthy life, you need to ensure that the environment you work or stay in is tidy and clean. Any kind of illness kills your schedule and wastes a lot of your time.

Set a hotspot for clutter in your house or office. The most notorious points are the kitchen sink, bedroom drawers, nightstands, and dining tables. These are the places you need to check every day. After work, take a few minutes in the shower to freshen up. This will ensure you get a good sleep.

6. Be Discipline to Your Deadlines and Schedules

Discipline is key when it comes to being organized. Laziness has no place here; they go hand in hand with productivity. Organized people will have a schedule for a day, a week, a month, and even a year. It is one thing to have one and another to strictly follow it.

Living a disorganized life makes it hard for you to meet your deadlines or achieve your goals. Try this: Write down whatever you want to achieve this year. After doing that, write down what you need to do to achieve those goals.

7. Set Your Priorities Right

For you to simplify your life, it is important to understand your priorities in life. Be conscious about your time. Identify what matters most to you and start working on them. You can never learn this from anybody; only you understand the most important thing in your life.

At times, you concentrate too much on the sideshows instead of dealing with the real issues. List down your day's, week's, or month's activities. List them down according to the most important. Time will never be enough to accomplish everything. If you fail to accomplish everything, at least ensure that those important activities have been accomplished.

8. Disregard Clutter

You do not need to complicate things in your life to be successful. After identifying the most important things, eliminate the unnecessary. Imagine a scenario where you are to permanently transfer with your family to a foreign country and you are told to take with you only the most important things. Stop for a moment and think. What would you carry with?

People tend to develop an emotional attachment to things that have been with them for a long time. There is that one car that has been in your garage for more than five years. You probably love it, and you fear getting rid of it. What is it doing there? Get rid of it to create space for your new car! Here are a few simple things you need to do to ensure everything you do.

9. Do a Quick Cleanup

There are two ways of doing this—the daily cleanup and the big cleanup every season. Pick a basket, go around your house, and pick up the dirt. This will not take more than ten minutes of your time.

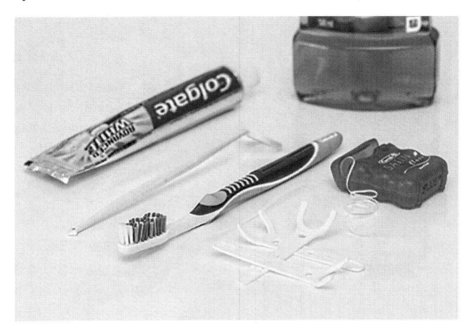

There is no excuse for not doing this. Once in a while, do a thorough cleaning, maybe three times a year—this depends on the situation of your place. You may be forced to hire or add a workforce to help. Go through your desks, drawers, and bedrooms and eliminate the unnecessary. Note that it is important to keep your documents in a soft form.

10. Shrink Your Wardrobe

Take a look at your wardrobe; it is probably full of clothes. Do you wear all of them? Certainly not. Sort your most versatile clothes and get rid of the rest. Those clothes could help someone somewhere. You could donate them to the unfortunate in society. Some people burn what they no longer need. It is not a good idea, and it is satisfying to know that, through your little effort, someone somewhere is smiling.

11. Buy Only the Things You Need

Suppose you were in a shopping mall and you found a nice item. Would you just pick it up? Impulse buying is not a good idea. If you feel you need it, put it down in your to-do list. Take a few days before deciding to buy it if you must purchase the item.

Myths behind Organizing and Strategizing Your Life

Many people have a wrong impression or perception of organizing and strategizing your life. By looking around or observing people in social media, you will be tempted to think that the only gateway to a successful, organized life is through having a million dollars in your bank account. It is important to get rid of these misconceptions by understanding what life is made of. Here are the eight myths surrounding being organized:

1. **"I need money to organize and simplify my life."** You don't need to purchase the most sophisticated equipment in your house to be organized. All you need to do is put everything in the right place. Unless necessary, you don't need to spend a coin in an effort to reorganize your life. Create a system that works for you. Put away the idea of copying others to make good of your life.

2. **"It does no matter where I keep my things."** Research shows that being organized goes hand in hand with productivity. Organized people are more likely to succeed compared to their colleagues. In your office, keeping various documents in different files helps in keeping the records safe. It will save you time.

3. **"Organizing will never work for me."** This is mostly contributed by self-esteem. It is important to trust your abilities since, just like others, you can also do it. All you need is willpower. This perception may have been contributed by people who constantly look at your downfalls. Everything has a

first time, and perhaps it is your time to start relooking at how you can strategize and organize your life.

4. **"My time for organizing and strategizing my life will come."** It is common for every person to want to postpone everything. That time will never come. Take that step and start taking charge of your life today. Before I took charge of my garage, I disliked visiting it because of its situation. Take a look at my garage after I took a step of reorganizing it. It is now one of the places I love visiting in my house.

5. **"Being organized is a one-day thing."** This is entirely wrong. Strategizing and organizing your life is an everyday thing. That said, there are different forms of organization—long-term and short-term organization. Short-term plans are done daily while the long-term ones are done once in a while.

6. **"Organizing is tedious and time-consuming."** A quote by a New York–based strategist says, "If you know the difference between a shirt and a pair of pants, you're halfway there." It is that simple! Contrary to that belief, the aftermath of organizing and strategizing saves you time. Adding up the time you will spend trying to think where you kept some item is a waste of time.

7. **"Being organized is an inborn trait."** This is an excuse used by lazy people to get away with their disorganization. Nobody is born organized; we all learn to take control of our life. I have seen people change from living a messed-up life to living a good and well-structured life. To prove that it is not an inborn thing, look around and see the people you admire. How are their lives moving? Even though it might not be true for all of them, most had their lives messed up before taking the step of changing their lives.

8. **"Being organized is being perfect."** Not even the best people you look up to in this world are perfect. The most important factor in life is knowing what you want. Plan to achieve it. Create the best strategic plan that works best for you. You can perform best within your environment. Many people fail while trying to be perfect. It is not about paperwork but the will to change your way of living. Life is like a work in progress that can never end. Every day we try to live a better life.

Chapter 2

The Ultimate Guide to Understanding What Matters Most

Have you ever taken a moment of thinking about what matters most in your life? The society we are living in has placed material things, like wealth, relationships, houses, or cars, as the things that matter most.

As I take you through this journey of understanding what matters most in life, the will to change your life is a personal decision. My aim is to guide you to understand the most important things that matter in life. Below are the six most important factors in life:

1. Stay true to yourself.

2. Remove the unnecessary clutter.

3. Plan your workouts.

4. Carry only the things you need.

5. Maintain good hygiene.

6. Stay true to yourself.

Strategies of Staying True to Yourself

Did you know that it is better to make the wrong decisions in life than compromising every decision in life? The most successful people in life are those people who stand for something. Trust your choices and move on. You will learn from your wrong choices. Here are some of the strategies that will help you stay true to yourself.

1. **Do not sacrifice what you stand for to please other people.** It is not an easy thing to do, considering the kind of world we are living in. People around us will always question some of the decisions we make. What you need to do is to stop and ask yourself a simple question: "Who is responsible for your choices?" It is you! That said, it does not mean that you stop listening to other people. Did you know that denying yourself what you want is not just self-sacrifice but also self-destruction? There is a misconception out there that differing with other people is a mistake. It is healthy to have a different opinion. Agree to disagree. A huge number of people fake their lives two make others happy. Often others never realize that they are living other people's lives. Parents take too much control over their children's lives. I have witnessed children who break down after the passing of their parents. They have no clue what to do without their parents.

2. **Be strict on your time and space.** Do you ever fear being alone? Or do you fear losing people you love? Despite this fact, being alone is one of the most important moments in our lives. It helps in meditation and in realizing the inner self in you. It is said that the more intelligent you get, the less you talk. The most intelligent people are the people who love being alone.

3. **Do not overdepend on other people.** Seeking help from other people is common. If this practice is overdone, it will come back to hurt us. People will start avoiding you, hence hurting your esteem. You will start feeling that you are a bother to people. Another important thing about overdependence on the people is that it brings laziness. In a situation where you are sure that whatever you do someone will always come to your aid, you will not push yourself enough to achieving your dreams.

4. **Every person's time of success varies.** You can never be someone else. Trust me, you will hurt yourself trying. Your path to success is different from my path. What you need to do is learn from my path—take the good and ignore the bad. There is a misconception that you should follow all that your role model does. Come on, you can never have everything your role model has achieved. The sole purpose of having a role model is to borrow the things he or she did in the aim of achieving their dreams.

5. **Never let other people make you feel guilty.** This is common for many people. Let people pay for their actions. Nobody forces anyone to make a decision; all you do is advice. Our advice at times does not go as expected. Not all advice goes as expected. It is, therefore, time to start feeling obligated to yourself. If anything happens to you, it is solely your life. All others can do is feel pity for you. They cannot change anything.

Twelve Reminders of the Things That Matter Most in Life

1. **Every minute counts.** In one of her quotes, Blaze Olamiday says, "Don't hesitate to live every moment out of your life in the best way you can because living is once, chances are rare, and nothing is certain." Another important factor in life is the will to accept our mistakes and learn from them to create a better future.

2. **Search your soul to find who you are.** Few people understand who they are. No one except yourself knows who you really are. To help you with this, look at your principles, the people you love hanging out with, and whatever you enjoy doing most. The three will help you understand who you are. "Be yourself. Everyone else is already taken'' (Oscar Wilde).

3. **Experience is what matters most.** Forget about what you read in books or what you learned from your mentors; the most

important factor is the experience. It is said that experience is the best teacher—this is entirely true. Only a fool will not learn a single thing from their past. Are you happy with the person you are now? A few people will answer yes to this question. If your answer is yes, you would not be interested in reading my book. If no, there is a reason behind it. The reason is your past experiences. It is, therefore, good to understand your past.

4. **Know what counts most.** Look at this wonderful quote from Mahatma Gandhi: "Your beliefs become your thoughts, your thoughts become your words, your words become your actions, your actions become your habits, your habits become your values, and your values become your destiny." Are your values acceptable in your society? Through religious institutions, schools, or even family, values are instilled to us. Values are what guide us to living a good life, not only for yourself but also for the society we are living in.

5. **Give and share with others with love.** This all begins by loving yourself. It is difficult to love others without loving yourself. Look at yourself every day in the mirror and say good things about yourself. At first, this will look weird, but trust me, it gives the much-needed confidence. It is through self-love that we can love others. Loving someone gives you strength and courage. Coexistence is key here if you want to live a good life. Learn to live well with others.

6. **Be happy.** Happiness is one of the most important factors in life. Happiness attracts happiness; it is through your happy moments that you realize the positive sides of your life. Putting too many worries to yourself will not change anything. As you take note of the things that are pulling you down in life, take a moment to celebrate the good moments in your life. Think about your family or your accomplishments. Take time to celebrate this moment.

7. **Remove the unnecessary clutter.** Clutter not only drains you physically; it is also an emotional factor. Every time you walk into your cluttered house or office, it kills your morale. Have you ever felt uncomfortable in your own house or feel guilty whenever someone visits you? Its time you start cluttering the items in your house. Why is it important to remove the unnecessary things in your life? Here is the reason: It takes away your focus. The unnecessary things in your house take away your focus. Instead of focusing on the real issues, your mind is diverted, hence wears down and your ability to focus. Research done from Princeton University indicates that everything that catches your sight competes for your attention. It is, therefore, advisable to make your place as tidy as possible to concentrate best at your working place.

8. **Remove clutter.** Scientists have proven that clutter spike your stress hormones. A study involved houses with abundant toys or household items and house without the mentioned items. Clutter has similarities with multitasking—both overload your brain. It makes you unnecessarily stressed and anxious. A research study done about mothers indicates that their stress levels on the thought of an untidy home. They were more relaxed when the house was left clean and organized in the morning. Unclutter your house every morning, and your day will be better.

9. **Clutter is costly.** Clutter robs you not only time but also money. Think about how your day has always been, looking for lost car keys every morning, a lost file in your computer, or even a misplaced paper in your office. Research has shown that Americans lose approximately 9 million hours every day looking for lost items. As if that is not enough, losing some items come with an additional cost of paying for the penalties involved.

10. **Having clutter might lead to an increase in body weight.** A rise in the stress levels increases your body weight. This is not, however, the case for everyone; stress decreases the body weight of others. Families with clutter are more likely to consume more food than their organized counterparts. It is because you are more likely to consume more food when exposed to them. Even though everyone has the urge to consume more food, people who are always exposed to more food will likely consume large amounts of food. The setup of your home or workplace is a reflection of your mind and body.

11. **Clutter holds you to the past.** Clutter traps you in the past according to the feng shui principle. The principle states that through clearing clutter in your place, you release the negative energy and develop positive energy. Also, clearing clutter opens the way for new opportunities in life. In her book *The Life-Changing Magic of Tidying Up*, Marie Kondō says to keep only the things that are close to your heart. Discard other things. By doing so, you can reset your life. You can also donate them to others who may need those items.

12. **No one cares about your stuff.** Are you feeling unwanted and lost? Does no one seem to give a damn about you? You are not alone; many people feel the same. The only reason why you think you are alone is that few people will come out to express this feeling. Never spend any second of your time worrying about people who don't care about you. They are not worth your time. By worrying about them, you are justifying their act of not caring about you. Ensure that they know that whatever they do is least of your concerns. Dismiss their opinions as silly and undeserving of your time. A picture of the United States president when asked about something sums how you should express things that do not bother you.

What You Should Do When You Feel You Are Alone

Know that it is a short-term feeling. It is important to know that the feeling is temporary. Therefore, it is important to choose your path. Take a moment and remind yourself of who you are. It is time for you to let go of the negative energy in your life.

Many times, you feel alone after a breakup or divorce. The feeling will be over faster than you think. If it is a breakup, do not rush into another relationship. Take as much time as possible to discover what you want.

Chapter 3

Set Your Goals
and Priorities Right

A goal is a personal achievement desired by a person within a given period. In other words, goals are long-term plans for the future with a given deadline. Most people start a day or year without a clear focus on long-term strategies to achieve their goals.

On the other hand, a small number of people begin their year or day with detailed goals. This is an important practice that will aid your success in life. Before sitting down to set these goals, first, understand your priorities and what you aim at achieving at the end of the year.

Before setting up the outline of your goals, consider the following factors, time, drive, and ability.

Definition of Success in Your Perspective

Success, simply put, is the state of having accomplished or achieved an aim or objective. The dictionary meaning is "attaining prosperity, wealth, and or fame." However, the true definition goes far beyond the common definition that the media has idolized time and time again. Wealth, degrees, tangible accomplishments, and money cannot be used as the yardstick with which we measure success. Consequently, the number of people whose lives you have positively influenced and who can live better lives because of something you created is a better description of success. To live a happy life defined by you and the ability to make the world you live in a better place is the true meaning of success.

The concept that we are all on the journey to create success implies that most (if not all) of us are aware what it means for us and that usually someone else has the key and ability to unlock it for us. This is as much a fallacy as it is a lie. Every one of us is unique, and while we all want to live a life that is socially acceptable, we have to understand that success should be defined just as unique as we are to each other. We have to find our definition of success and own it.

For some of us, this means buying your dream car, getting that promotion that you imagine will change your life, settling down with your significant other, and starting a family or traveling the world. For many, success is tied to a financial goal, and others a health and fitness goal. The point is that your definition of success does not necessarily match someone else's. Success is as personal as your fingerprint, and understanding how other people measure success can help you know how you gauge it for yourself.

Success doesn't have to be something set on a grand scale, and usually, that's where we go wrong. You can succeed in smaller things, and the addition of these little victories is what leads to the achievement of the grand plan. After all, one must crawl before they can walk and then run. Similarly, success doesn't equate to perfection. Since life is not static, you should not set your goals in a manner that does not allow for flexibility. More often than not, there are diversions, failures, and disappointments. Eventually, you will get to where you want to be if you're set on your sights, that is.

Success is largely individual. When we compare ourselves with our neighbors, we get frustrated because we feel like our colleagues have it more figured out that we do. The irony is that they're probably thinking the very same way about us. Comparison usually comes from a place of lack. The more we focus on our inadequacies, the more likely we are to feel like we are to miss out on the great things we already have going great for us. We eventually end up adopting the mantra that "we are not yet successful," all the while comparing our lives to someone else's idea of success.

What Is Success in Your Perspective?

What metric do you use to define success? Many of us are hardwired to define success regarding what we can see and touch. We believe that success is external. We define success by how we are perceived by other people, the way we look and act, the cars we drive, and the praise we get for the things we have acquired. The problem with this is that if these tangible things are lost, we sink into depression.

We spend so much time chasing validation from others, eventually fashioning our lives in a way that we consider socially acceptable while deep down we crave the simple things—to be loved and accepted. Pleasing and proving are exhausting as we soon discover. Acquiring one thing will only lead you to want another and another to no end. We will never feel fully validated by physical things because there is always a newer, bigger, and better version. The question is "Until when?" At what point does it stop? When is it enough?

The answer is "Never." Until we turn our eyes inward, we will always be stuck chasing fleeting things and dangerous highs.

To find success, you need to start looking within. Psychologists have found that those who look within themselves for success have reported higher senses of fulfillment, happiness, and general satisfaction toward life. This is as it should be. Intrinsic goals are the name of this type of success. They are much more satisfying and permanent because they are set out to feed a psychological need.

Examples are things that relate to personal growth, giving back to the community, giving and ultimately receiving more love. The next time you feel frustrated and stagnant as far as success is concerned, you need to stop and shift the work within. You are more successful than you believe.

Success is achieved by having a plan or a goal. You need to set and write down your goals. Define a strategy for which you will achieve it and follow through. You need to understand that unlike popular belief, success is more of the journey than it is a destination. By sticking to your goals and having a conscious effort to tick off the items, you will soon realize that your life will turn for the best even if you have not achieved much as far as physical possessions go. Again, it's all in the mind.

Importance of Setting Goals in Life

The way you live your life solely depends on the actions you take daily. You are responsible for your life. We like to look outward and blame our circumstances on external forces and other people, but this should not be the case. At this very moment, do you know what you want to achieve and how you intend on achieving it? If the answer is no, how then will you know when and if you get there? The main difference between dreams and goals is that dreams are just that, dreams. Goals, however, are a step-by-step guide on how to achieve something. Everything in existence was once a thought in someone's mind, an idea that was planned out and brought into fruition.

In mind, you have all the thoughts, dreams, and plans of what you want to do, who you want to be, the things you want to achieve, and the ways we want to change the lives of those around us. The problem is that without a solid plan, we don't change much, either within or without. We need goals to change our situations.

1. Goals Give You a Focus

Imagine having a bow and arrow and then being asked to shoot without being given a target. Where would you aim at, and why would you aim at that particular spot? What would be the purpose of doing it, to begin with? This is the idea of living life without a goal; it is a pointless waste of energy and valuable time.

Say your goal is to set up a pastry business. Although you don't have a clue about where to start, having it as a goal is enough to focus your thoughts and energy into this venture. You then brainstorm ideas on how to start. You first study the pastry business in your community

26

and the brands that the society associates most with. You then find a local pastry school and sign up to hone your skills. Soon you start to make your pastries and get your friends to sample them. Little by little, your goal materializes, and soon you have a small pastry shop.

Consider your energy as the input and the results as the output. A goal creates a focal point for you to channel your energy. You can have all the ambition in the world, but without having a place to focus it on, it won't have much difference. You need to focus your efforts on a goal because, at the end of the day, goals give us direction. Allowing your mind to focus on a specific target will provide you with the best results instead of aimlessly expending energy on some scattered and unrelated activities.

2. Goals Hold You Accountable

It is impossible to evaluate progress if you do not know what your goals are. Writing down your goals gives you something measurable against the time you had slotted. It is humbling to look at your goals a year or two later and realize that you had the potential to achieve more than you did. This is a clear indication that the system you're using is not working. This could be because it doesn't fit your situation and that you need to make changes.

Setting and writing down your goals is a tangible proof that you are obligated to act to correct the situation. This is being accountable to yourself and nobody else. It's the best kind actually because, in as much as we can give excuses to other people, we cannot lie to ourselves. Only you know the potential that you have. We may have people in our lives that understand what we are capable of, but at the end of the day, it boils down to what we know deep down.

3. Goals Enable You to Live Your Life to the Fullest

Setting goals allows you to live life to the maximum. Every moment and every action is geared toward our goal; hence, you have to make the most out of every situation. There is a lot to experience and so much life to live, but nothing is going to be handed to us unless we work for it.

Imagine being on vacation in an exotic country. With so much to see and endless places to visit, wouldn't you want to have a plan for the places you want to visit? You would want to research ahead on the activities you will engage in. Would you rather aimlessly wander the streets, hoping something interesting crosses your path? The latter mindset would lock you out of so much experience. Life is like a vacation in some ways, although it usually doesn't feel like it. You have been handed a limited amount of time to experience it, and before you know it, time is up. To bet the most out of our experience in life, eliminating the possibility of regrets, you have to be fully aware of exactly what you want.

This should not be taken to mean that every little action has to be planned out. Goals are the grand plan with which we live life, not the rule book. There is, of course, a little wiggle room for serendipity. As you check off one thing or the other, you will come to realize that some goals aren't actually what you want, and as time goes by, your list will get edited over and over. As you grow older, your destination will change as you come to terms with who you are and what you want. This is healthy. Without a clear goal, you may miss out on the beauty of what life has to offer. After all, this is a journey, not a destination.

4. Staying True to Your Goals

You have most likely heard the expression "Be true to who you are." This is an expression that you need to keep as a mantra. It doesn't matter what situation you are in. You may be working for a certain company where you have a few expectations from your boss. The work environment requires that you alter some aspects of yourself to get the promotion, to keep the job, or to be socially acceptable at the workplace. Attempting to please everyone will jeopardize your values and ultimately cause internal conflict.

Remaining focused on your goals is a hard task. We are certainly motivated at the beginning, but as time goes, the motivation wanes. Daily routines and tasks get in the way. We get overloaded with responsibility and distracted. This causes us to veer off-track as far as our goals go, and keeping track becomes an uphill task.

Important Determinants for Setting Your Goals

1. Time

How much time is available to achieve your goals? Time is an important factor in a person's life. Every activity is dictated by time. Be a realist. Set goals that are achievable within the available timeline. The moment you set deadlines that are not within your timelines, you will quickly lose morale after realizing that your goals are unattainable.

2. Ability

You are the only person who knows what you are capable of and what you cannot achieve. When setting your goals, be careful not to set up things that will surpass your abilities. A friend of mine's resolution was reaching the peak of Mt. Everest. The goal went on to be a failure since he has a heart condition that cannot sustain such weather condition. Thus, it is important to measure your abilities before setting your goals.

3. Motivation

Before setting up your goals, it is important to consider what drives you toward setting those goals. This is basically how far you are willing to go to achieve your goals. There should be a strong will to achieving your goals. Can you imagine setting up a goal of reading fifty novels by the end of the year when you cannot even complete reading one novel? You are not a fan of reading. Your goals should go hand in hand with what you love doing.

4. Consequences

As you sit down to set your goals and priorities, consider the impact they will have in your life. While some activities may seem exciting, their aftermath may not be too good. A perfect example is setting a goal to spend more hours in your workplace with the aim of increasing your productivity. Even though the goal may look good on paper, think about its impact on your family. Nobody would want to lose their family. The sacrifice is not worth it.

Staying focused on your goals is hard. In the beginning, we're certainly motivated. But we all know how that motivation wanes over time. We get caught up, stuck, frustrated, overloaded, overworked, and distracted. We simply veer off-track. It's hard to stay focused when we have so much going on.

Whenever obligations stretch us thin, it's straightforward to let life overwhelm us. It's easy to let emergencies and events that feel insurmountable shadow our goals and make our efforts feel a bit unimportant. These excuses may feel justifiable at the moment, but we know that they will only take us so far. Keeping track of our goals is important. Staying focused is not only essential but also crucial.

More often than not, trying to mold yourself to fit into other people's desires and views will leave you in an internal conflict that will stretch into our lives with family members, loved ones, and acquaintances.

What Do You Truly Want?

We usually carry with us certain beliefs and notions without ever stopping to ask ourselves if they are what we want. We fail to determine if they are a true reflection of who we are or if they fit into what we believe to be true in life. These beliefs box us in notions of fearing what others may think if we truly reveal ourselves.

You may want to have that big car or that house or the promotion. These are all fine if they are what we want. Are you true to yourself, or do you desire these things because of the socially acceptable notion you have of yourself? If you find yourself being a different person at work than you are at home or with your friends, it's time to ask yourself, "Is this what I want, or is it what is expected of me? What is keeping me from being myself?"

Let Your Personality Shine

The most beautiful people are those who let their true selves out without fear. They exude warmth, joy, and confidence. You will realize that in so doing, these people naturally give those around them the freedom to express their true selves. People feel comfortable around them, and as a result, the beauty spreads out. Know such people? If you don't, you just might be it.

The happiest and most successful people follow their dreams. They have the confidence to pursue their heart's desire. They have so much faith in themselves and what they are about what others can't fail to believe in them too.

As this year looms ahead, ask yourself if you're doing what you dreamed of all along. Ask yourself if you'll be happy at the close of the year with how you lived your life. Are there any changes you wanted to make last year that you didn't? Is there anything that you are sure you will regret not doing? Life may be short, but it is also the most extended experience we will ever have. It will be a waste to go through it living within someone else's standards. Be true to yourself. Do not be afraid to express the amazing person that you are.

Create Effective Habits

Sound habits are necessary for long-term success. Many of the tasks that we do every day are habits, and they may either make or break us. Some of these habits have been with us since childhood and may be hard to break. The most fundamental thing is to create habits that will ultimately draw you closer and closer to your goal.

Replace any negative habits with more creative ones. It may prove to be a challenging task, but persistence will eventually pay off. Persistence will ingrain the new habit until with time you will realize that you do not need a conscious effort to stay on track. At this point, you will know that you have beaten the old habit. Do this with every single one that you dislike, and you will recreate yourself. Stop habits like procrastinating, aimlessly surfing the net, and wasting precious time on social media.

Be Accountable to Someone

You might be laser-focused and disciplined, but I advocate that you be accountable to someone. This may be a mentor, a spouse, business partner, or a friend. Being accountable to someone will help you remain focused. We have only ourselves to answer to regarding our goals. Regardless of this, it helps to have someone look in from the outside and gauge your progress with you.

We need some motivation every once in a while. Be sure not to confuse motivation with fishing for compliments. These two are not interchangeable. The person you are accountable to will be able to tell you when you are slacking and give you a pat for a job well done.

It is advisable to work with someone who has walked your path and knew you. This person should be able to give you impartial advice and a perspective that is unbiased.

Define the Word "Complete"

Know when you are done. In your journey, you need to clearly define when a task is complete and when it needs more work. You will find that in some instances you will add little tasks to an already existing one. This will postpone the completion date of the task that you have at hand. Nothing is worse than a perpetual task. If you realize that more work crops up about what you are already doing, take note of this and have a plan for it as well.

Micro-tasks are not healthy as they prolong the life of a goal and ultimately kill your morale for it. In the end, you may not even recognize where you started or even be clear about a definitive ending. Don't leave room for micro-tasks to crop up into your existing tasks. Just add new ones and define a completion time for them.

Being a Realist

As much as we should aim at the sun to reach the moon, you should aim at finding the middle ground between not high enough and too high. If you set goals that you are sure of not attaining, trust me, you will get tired of even trying. Some goals are continuous while some have specific timelines. In general, a good goal is one that is worthy of your effort and time. No one should ever set your goals for you since you are the only one who knows your abilities.

In the current world, your attitude can either make or break you. Most people categorize everyone else as being either an optimist or pessimist, which is rather limiting. If you believe that the glass is either half empty or half full, you eliminate the option that the glass could also be full or empty.

Realists are people who know how to make sense of the world, which is a big advantage. The world views realists as being closer to pessimists who downplay every good thing and consider the bad as inevitable. In essence, a realist is someone who sees things as they are. The realist does not apply any kind of filter, either positive or negative, to any situation. Generally, a realist is unbiased in every way.

A realist sees the world as it is. As a realist, you see the truth and nothing else. You are not swayed by idealistic aims and unconscious bias that move most people. Conversely, you see things in their truth and prefer them to be unvarnished.

Successful Tips for Setting Your Goals

It is not about achieving your goal but what you do to achieve your goals. Through setting your goals, you become focused, and your life is shaped. I will take you through successful tips that will help you in setting your goals. The mention of goals can be intimidating. Just think of goals as a to-do list with a given dateline. The difference, however, is that goals keep changing as time passes. On the way, some are added, and others are subtracted.

1. Set Your Goals in Accordance with Priorities

Top priorities should be about yourself, not your spouse, child, or employer. Remember, you are priority number one in life. The moment you let other people the first priority in life, you will be sabotaging your own future. Your second priority will probably be your family before others.

2. Put Your Goals in Writing

The moment you put your goals on paper, they will sound real. You will also be binding to your future since you can never remove whatever you have written. When writing down your goals, remember to use a decisive language. Instead of using phrases like "I would," use "I will." Using such a language will show how serious you are about implementing your goals.

Some phrases show your will and power to achieve your goals. Another important factor is posting your goals in a visible place, like walls or desk, to serve as a constant reminder. You might be thinking that goals are supposed to be a secret. No, what you want your life to be like is not a secret. You should not be ashamed of what you want your life to be like.

3. Make Reasonable and Measurable Goals

Only you know your abilities. You know what you can achieve by the end of the year or by the end of five years.

Do not generalize whatever you want to achieve. Be specific on your timelines. For instance, if one of your goals is purchasing a car, be specific on the kind of vehicle you want to buy. Consider your timeline and the amount of money you can raise within your stipulated timeline.

4. Flexibility Is Key

"Only a fool is never ready to change his mind." This common phrase applies to your goals. If you come across better ideas along the way, never hesitate to alter your goals. Priorities keep changing daily. At times, opportunities that will enable you to achieve your dreams within a short period present themselves. Grab those opportunities without hesitating. Keep in mind that an opportunity never presents itself twice but only once in a lifetime.

5. Your Goals Should Be Relevant

You must be familiar with the importance of setting your goals. As much as it may sound like a cliché, it is important to talk about them.

Before setting your goals, consider your family life and career. What direction do you want your life to take is the basic question you are supposed to ask yourself. Some goals could mess up your life instead of helping. Also, setting fluttered and inconsistent goals could scatter your life.

Chapter 4

Develop a Work Formula
(The 50/30/20 Rule)

Y ou know how much money you earn. You have reviewed your budget and are aware of the amount of money you spend on different things in life. That is all fine, although this usually leaves questions about other things, like emergency savings. How does your financial situation compare to the amount of money you should put aside for saving?

The 50/30/20 rule, coined by Elizabeth Warren, discusses the nitty-gritty of spending and saving.

1. **Needs—50 percent of your income.** The things that you must take care of fall in this category. These are rent, groceries, car payments, gas, health, insurance, and phone bills. Things like Netflix, dining out, and the occasional Starbucks do not fall in this category. You allot the first 50 percent to this category. This may seem like so much of your income, but it will start to make sense once you consider the things that fall into this category. This category lets you adjust depending on your essential needs but remains a sound and balanced budget.

2. **Personal wants—30 percent of your income.** Wants are the things that you spend money on, although they are not necessarily essential. This is where movies, dining out, and HBO come in. This category also houses the upgrades that you make, like premium accounts or choosing a prime steak at dinner over the regular. Only you can decide what expenses to

slot in this category. These are the things you choose that make life a bit more entertaining and enjoyable for you. To this category, you should allot 30 percent of your earnings. Mind you, these are calculated after you have deducted your income tax, so keep that in mind. This category gets a higher allotment than your savings because of the sheer number of things that fall into it. Of course, this varies for different people. The fewer choices you have in this section, the more money you will have left over to pay off debts and save to secure your future.

3. **Savings—20 percent of your income.** The final step is to dedicate 20 percent to your investments and savings. This includes funds stowed away for a rainy day, debt payments, and savings plans. This category includes things that you could do but do not necessarily endanger your life if you didn't. Even though the term "retirement" doesn't carry a lot of weight when you are only twenty-four, it certainly does as you get a bit older. You will be glad you started early, trust me. Making this category is a step to ensuring a stress-free future.

Why it works: This is an excellent place to start if you are unsure about how to generally spend your income. By breaking your spending into these categories, you will have covered your goals, obligations, and indulgences.

When it doesn't: This plan might prove difficult for you if you cannot differentiate between wants and needs. Fifty percent toward housing and bills might be a bit too much for you if you live in a low-cost area. However, if you live in a high-rise location and most of your indulgences and bills are paid for by your job, then this rule might seem quite ambiguous for you.

The point is to use it to tailor your situation. Design something that fits your income and lifestyle. You might find that by applying this rule, you have been spending a bit too much in one area without realizing it. This can ultimately help you make some life decisions, like maybe moving houses, living closer to your work, or cutting down on expenses whenever you can.

Develop a Capsule Wardrobe

If you find yourself getting exhausted by the sheer number of decisions that you have to make on a daily basis, you are in good company. A lot of people—notable ones, like Barrack Obama and Steve Jobs—have admitted to being weighed down by the decision of what to wear every single day. This finally led them to just wearing essentially the same thing. Dwelling on little decisions every other day could leave you indecisive and exhausted at the end of the day. Enter the capsule wardrobe.

A capsule closet is a small collection of clothes, shoes, and accessories that help you live a simple and easy life. It reduces the options we have on what to wear by its minimalistic principle. Aside from eliminating decision fatigue, the capsule wardrobe has many other benefits as well. It eliminates the shopaholic habit, enables you to understand your style better, and save closet space and time.

A capsule closet essentially consists of around thirty to fifty pieces of clothing as your entire wardrobe for a specific period. These are the clothes that complement each other and are also fully functional. Having a capsule wardrobe means getting rid of the allure of spending more on your wardrobe. It is based on the principle of less is more, meaning you will only own the clothes that you constantly wear. This motivates you to pick high-quality pieces that will hold over time and serve you better.

Additionally, with fewer choices to rummage through, your dressing time goes from a half hour to three minutes. Spending less on clothing will enable you to channel that extra coin into a savings account or something productive, like a new hobby.

Whereas the capsule wardrobe is not a new concept, its popularity has surged within the past few years. Fashion bloggers across the internet have popularized it by talking about their own experiences trying it. Here are the ways of making it work for you:

1. Take stock of your wardrobe. Since you are going to live with a few selected items for the next few months, it is advisable to choose these pieces wisely. You need to take a serious look into what you're wardrobe holds. You know the things you wear often and those that you hoard with the promise that you might need them someday. Seriously, though, how often do you need that hoodie at the bottom of your closet?

2. Choose the pieces that are going into the capsule. Stock your capsule with about forty pieces that include shoes, skirts, blouses, blazers, and dresses. Note that gym clothes, sleepwear, underwear, and clothes that you work out in should not go into your capsule. Anything that you wear on special occasions has no place in here either; they are considered freebies.

3. Give it a three-month trial. Upon picking out your capsule wardrobe, you're ready to live it. Do not deviate from anything in your capsule. There is a reason that you chose what you chose. Be disciplined enough to wear only what is in your capsule and, of course, some free-pass items like nightwear and underwear for a straight three months. Some parts of this will be easy, while some things might prove difficult. There might be some things you moved that was your favorite. Even if the process proves difficult, the point is to brave it out and stick with the rules. You will learn more about your style and even get creative when it comes to matching the items you have in the capsule.

4. Start over. Congratulations on sticking it out! Once you near the end of the three months, evaluate what worked and what didn't. Did you wish you had more color variety, or discover that you don't wear heels as much? These little assessments will eventually give you a glimpse of what is important. You

might find that some items in your full closet are no longer desirable and you can turn them in for a few bucks or donate them. Ultimately, this task is aimed at reducing clutter and helping you prioritize on clothing.

Make Your Lunch the Night before Work

The best way to save money and have a nutritious meal is by packing your lunch. This is especially handy if your mornings are particularly hectic. You might skip packing a lunch box or maybe forget to do so entirely. Doing so the night before, when you have a bit more time, is much easier.

The average lunch costs between $7 and $13. Packing lunch saves you so much more. This is because more often than not, we usually pack what was left over from dinner or what we already have sitting in the fridge. Separate the leftovers into meal-sized portions in your fridge so that all you have to do is grab one and go.

Packed lunches give you flexibility and push you to be creative. If you do not have a cooked meal, you can assemble a few items in your fridge. Wondering what to do with that piece of chicken? Make a chicken sandwich! Aside from this, packed lunches help you manage your weight because you get to pack in as many whole foods as possible. We all know that every time we eat out, we tend to indulge in our guilty pleasure, which is ultimately unhealthy in the long run.

Considerations: Since this is food that will sleep in the fridge and wait until lunch the next day, you need to be very hygienic about how you go about preparing it. Store the food in the refrigerator through the night and before you have to eat it. If your workplace doesn't have a fridge, freeze a bottle of juice or water and place it near your lunch. This will not only keep your food cool, but by the time lunch rolls in, the liquid will have thawed and will be an added beverage. Win-win.

By packing your lunch and having it in the cafeteria, you save a lot of time that you would have otherwise gone out looking for lunch. You can catch up on your mail, read a book, or surf the net while you eat. You will come to realize that this alone time is very beneficial, and with time, you will look forward to them.

New Information Is Power

The twenty-first century is referred to by many as the century of information. There has never been a time when information was so free-flowing and virtually free for that matter. The advent of e-books means that we no longer need to visit our local library to look something up. The click of a button is the difference between knowing something and total ignorance. The internet has been revolutionary as far as information access goes.

Still, with all this information flying around us, most of us do not know the difference between information and knowledge. The internet, which is the hub of a lot of information, is widely abused. You find yourself reading and absorbing so much information while surfing, but at what cost? The question is "What exactly are you reading?" Since information is power, some of it is useless. The problem is that it is the useless kind that is most captivating. You have to be wise when it comes to choosing what you consume.

The success of your endeavors lies entirely on the kind of information you have and mostly what you do with it. If you find that you have information on your hands that could affect your business but do nothing about it, it is useless to you. Regardless of whether the data is regarding your business, a new business venture, a potential client or contract, the data must be shared with the right people and responded to as quickly as possible. If you don't act on it, someone else will.

We get information when we are hungry and curious about it. Nothing knocks at our door. Curiosity is drawing things that are interesting and ultimately useful to us. When we notice the changes that are happening in the world around us and take action to get into the loop, we create a chain reaction that will put us at the top of the chain. We become the very first adopters of new technology and, as a result, become successful. Curiosity goes hand in hand with courage.

No coward was ever successful. That is why you need to be able to discern useful information from white noise. You need to build meaningful knowledge. It opens our eyes to interesting gaps in the ecosystem that other people have missed. You need to be aware of your niche and the opportunities in it. This comes from knowing where you are, the opportunities that you have, and the chances you have for growth. A person learning to play the guitar will be hearing more nuances in guitar notes than someone who doesn't. You have to start accumulating knowledge to be creatively curious.

When you are on a mission to find the meaning of life, the chances are that you will see it in something that unleashes your natural self. This will unleash your curiosity and brilliance.

Be Fair to Yourself

Often you are too hard on yourself. Look in the mirror and see the important creature that you are. You have spent all your life appreciating others while forgetting that you also need to be appreciated. Here are things you need to know about life:

1. **You matter more than you think.** It all starts with yourself. If you don't love yourself, no one will love you the way you want. Another important factor is the way you treat others. What you give is what you will get—always keep that that in mind. Do not wait to hear from people to understand your worth in life. No one is in this world without a purpose.

2. **Nothing happens for no reason.** This will sound kinda weird, but it is true. There is a reason why you are feeling neglected. It could be a fulfillment or a lesson for you from God. It may be a signal for you to take the right path of life. On the other hand, the feeling of being neglected is a show of bravery from you. Not many people are able to face such feeling head-on. Often

people will live in denial of the fact that they are unwanted in society. They end up compromising their values to impress those that do not love them. Never force someone to love you.

3. **The truth is not far from you.** Yes! It all starts with acceptance. The fact that you have accepted that people do care about you is a step toward healing. The feeling does not feel right, I know, but trust me, you are on the right path. All you need to do is listen to those small voices inside you. Time for yourself is, therefore, an important factor here. Go somewhere silent where you are alone. Open your heart to nature. Whether you believe it or not, someone out there is listening.

4. **There is light at the end of the tunnel.** I know how it feels to be alone on this earth. It is a sad feeling. Cases of suicide have been reported across the world on people facing rejection from their loved one. The worst feeling is when this feeling comes from people you love or family members. I spent most of my childhood moving from one foster home to another. It is not that I had no parents; they were both alcoholics. Trust me, it is a devastating feeling. The moment I discovered my purpose on earth, all the feeling of rejection disappeared. I have no grudge against my parents since it was through their rejection that I found my worth on this earth.

Put Your Own Feeling on Paper

The moment you keep your emotions bottled up, you will break at some point. Let it out! The best way to do that is through writing. Put your work out there as an anonymous writer, probably on social media. You will find out that you are not alone; many people can relate to how you feel.

Note that food, alcohol, sex, or even social media can fill that hole. Many take refuge in religion, which is not a bad idea. The answer, however, lies with you. Accept your self-worth and move on.

Plan Your Workouts

Do any movements that involve your muscles and burn calories. The most common activities include jogging, dancing, swimming, and running.

Increase your life span; start exercising today. Workout is one of the most important factors in a person's life regardless of sex, age, and physical ability. Exercise is the most common and healthy ways of weight control. Through burning calories, you can shed some weight. Workout does not necessarily involve rigorous exercises. Simple activities like just walking are equally important.

Visiting the gym regularly is important, and any kind of activity on the body is equally important. You can do simple activities such as walking to work, avoiding the elevator, using the stairs, and doing house chores. The most important factor in exercise is consistency. Conditions such as blood pressure and cardiovascular diseases are directly connected to exercising. Through workouts, your blood will flow smoothly. Workout also decreases the cholesterol levels in the body.

Tips for Setting Your Goals

Goals help you stretch your abilities and grow in ways you never imagine. Life is designed in a way that we dream for the future and live for today. The more powerful our goals will be, the more powerful we future will turn out to be.

To come up with a more organized way of setting your goals, here are tips that will help you in setting your goals in a proper and well-structured manner. Here are the tips that will help you in setting your goals appropriately.

Seeing through your goals for a long period is one of the most difficult things. During the initial stages of implementation, you will probably be motivated, and you give it your all. As time pass by, things start to change. You will be frustrated, stuck, and overloaded. You will probably veer out of track. When you have too much going on in mind, staying focused is relatively difficult. Do not allow such situations to overwhelm you. Stay focused and keep going.

Keep in mind that nothing you will ever want to achieve comes easy. You will have to toil hard for you to achieve your goals. If you want to know how hard it is to achieve your goals, look around and see the number of successful people in society. The number explains it all. With the right plan and focus, your path to success will be much easier.

1. Goals Will Keep You Focused

Imagine doing something without a focus or aim. How would you start doing it? What is the motivation behind whatever you are doing? I have seen many people with a lot of potentials in life but end up failing simply because they lack a good work plan. Through goals, you have a given direction to follow. Imagine walking through a path you are not sure of its direction. Think about the amount of time you waste looking for the right direction.

The sense of being sure of the direction your life is taking makes you focused on the real issues rather than wasting your time on sideshows. It allows you to predict where your life will be within a stipulated period. It is said that when you aim at nothing, you will hit at nothing.

2. You Can Measure Your Progress

Having clear goals in life allows you to measure your progress from time to time. Before writing a book, I begin drafting a work plan that will guide me throughout my journey. My work plan will constantly remind me if I am in the right direction or not. Am I still on the stipulated timelines? How many chapters am I left with? How much time do I have before I complete writing the book?

Imagine a scenario where you work aimlessly. You wake up every day without knowing what to do. You will fail terribly. First, you will end up repeating some activities and/or forget others along the way. Setting goals are not only meant for the end product; it also represents a process or a pathway that reminds you of what you strive to achieve.

3. Goals Keep You Away from Distraction

A well-defined goal keeps you away from distractions. Imagine a scenario where you plan on seeing off your girlfriend after work. You are supposed to be out of work at 5:00 p.m. The plane is taking off at 6:00 p.m., and so you have thirty minutes to reach the airport and thirty minutes to have a small chat with her. With such a schedule, you will not be distracted by anything. Goals have the same purpose. They dictate your schedule, hence keeping you from distraction. Once you set your goal, give it 100 percent. It is the only way to succeed in life.

4. Goals Help You to Avoid Procrastination

You are accountable to your goals. A task scheduled to be completed within a given date must be completed no matter the circumstances. On the flip side, imagine life without a game plan. You choose the tasks you want to do, and nothing motivates you to complete the task. Goals are constant reminders on what you are supposed to do. In case you fail in any of them, you will be aware that you are supposed to work harder to catch up.

Many people are not good with a deadline, and many times you tend to think that three months or one year is a long period. The best practice is to set long-term and short-term goals. The short-term goals will help you to strictly follow your deadlines while the long-term goals will help you in evaluating your progress.

5. Goals Act as a Motivation

What drives you in life? What is the motivation behind your hard work? The answers to these questions are the goals you want to achieve within a given period. Even though the road to achieving your goals will look difficult, think more about the endpoint rather than the journey. They provide a foundation on what you are set to do to achieve a given result. You will be able to focus your energy in the right direction.

Goals connect you to your innermost desires. It is a powerful driver of life since they act to strive for something. The beautiful things you would love to achieve are what keeps you moving. One of Henry Ford's quotes states that "obstacles are those frightful things you see when you take your eyes off your goal."

6. Goals Create Accountability

Evaluating your progress from time to time is important. Life is not just about talk. Start taking action by implementing all your projects within time. Always remember that every progress you make in life is a benefit to you first before anyone else. If you are not on the right track, your goals will help you in bringing you back to track.

Take for instance my journey as a writer; I set my weekly target, which I am accountable for. At the end of every week, I monitor my progress. I will improve on the things I was not able to accomplish in the previous week as I set myself to the next week. Through time, I have been able to grow as a writer. Start being accountable for every action you take in life.

7. Goals Help You Be the Best Person You Can Be

Did you know that more than 95 percent of people use less than 20 percent of their potential? Through goals, you can achieve your highest potential. Life without a goal keeps you in a comfort zone; you will not feel obligated to doing anything. It denies you the chance of making you achieve your potential.

Goals help you in stretching your abilities beyond the normal heights. A perfect example is marathoners. In their race, they are aware that by one hour, they should have clocked certain kilometers. Do not settle for anything less when setting your goals. Your guide should be the desires you strive to achieve.

8. Goals Ensure That You Live Your Best Life

Keep in mind that at the end of every year, you will be a year older. Life is too short to live without a purpose. Setting up goals ensures that you maximize your potential on earth. Once you discover your purpose in life, goals will help you fulfill your purpose. Before sitting down to set up your goals, consider factors like what you love most, your abilities, and the time frame you need to implement your goals.

Ways of Staying Focused on Your Goals

Life is a struggle. You wake up every morning for workouts, eat healthy, or work to beat your deadline. At some point, you feel like quitting. The solution, however, is not quitting. Think about the end product. It is important to ensure that every step you make takes you closer to your goals. Without extra effort and sacrifices, achieving your stipulated goals will be difficult. To make it in life, avoid unnecessary excuses.

1. Create a Mission Statement

Just like companies, you need a mission statement that will direct you toward things that matter. What are the things you believe in? What is your definition of success? If you have failed before, what will you change so as not to repeat the same mistakes? Your mission statement will be around four to five pages. It should be simple and should be placed in places where you can easily see it. Whenever you feel confused about life, go through your mission statement several times. It will bring you back on track.

2. Quit Overthinking and Start Working

This is common for most people. You spend too much time thinking instead of putting your acts together and start working. I remember my 2018 goal was to keep fit and be able to run around the house with my kids. Instead of working out on a plan to implement my goal, I began thinking too much about it. I ended starting my workout five months later. It is time to quit thinking and start working.

3. Keep Visualizing about the End Product, Not the Process

How would you feel like when you achieve your goals? How would life be like? These are common questions you need to ask yourself to stay motivated. If you keep thinking about the process or whatever you will go through to achieve your goals, it will demoralize you. It is like stopping by a gas station to fuel your car after a long journey. When you are almost giving up, take time to think about your life's desires and what you will do without them.

4. Always Look at the Bigger Picture

Always remember that it is not about finishing today's job; it is bigger than that. Often after accomplishing a certain job, you celebrate too much, forgetting that there is a tomorrow. As if that is not enough, you go drinking yourself up. Too much drink in the name of celebration reduces your tomorrow's potential.

5. Never Forget the Reason for Setting Your Goals

Sometimes in life, things will look too tough for you. In such a scenario, lie back and ask yourself why you took that path in the first place. If the reasons for choosing to take that road are not convincing enough, consider relooking at your goals. Goals are your motivation when things get tough. They will help you in clarifying issues during the worst moments.

6. Consistency Is Key

When you wake up every day to do the same thing, results must come your way. Hard work pays. Do not only work when you feel like it, but it should also be an everyday thing. Ensure you complete today's task to avoid giving yourself pressure of trying to catch up in the coming day.

7. Analyze Your Progress Every Day

Keep track of your progress. At times, you think you are doing too much, but on the real sense, you are behind schedule. This will help you in knowing whether to increase your effort or to continue at the same pace. This mostly applies to goals that are quantifiable, such as weight goals, money goals, and any other goal that can be measured in terms of numbers.

With the new technology all over the place, it has become an easy task to keep track of your daily activities. You can use your smartphone, iPad, or laptop to evaluate your progress. This will help you determine whether you have been doing the right thing or just wasting time.

Why It Is Important to Set Realistic Goals

Much as it is important to set goals in life, make sure your goals are attainable. Once you start setting unrealistic goals, prepare yourself for failure. Only you know your capabilities. Make your own goals; no one should ever dictate you on what your goals should be. I remember my parents making goals during my secondary school education. I tried too much and ended up losing hope since I was sure of not achieving them. Had I been given a chance to set my own goals, I am sure I would have performed better. Here is the reason why you should set your own goals: *to get rid of expectation.*

This does not mean that you should not trust your abilities. It means that you should not be blinded that you can do everything. Setting goals that are unrealistic are like setting yourself up for a disappointment. Do not set yourself up to purchase a car by the end of the year when you know that even if you save the whole of your income, it is not enough to purchase a car.

Evaluate Your Abilities before Setting Your Goal

1. **Be aware of the limitation.** It is important to put into consideration everything that can hinder you from achieving your goals. This limitation is internal while others are external. Internal limitations are caused by you, and you have control over them. External limitations, on the other hand, are things you do not have control over. Being aware of such restrictions will help you in dealing with them.

2. **Be specific in your goals.** It is important to be specific when setting your goals. Point out those particular things you want to achieve within a specific period. Do your research on the amount of time you need and, if money is involved, the total cost involved. Generalizing your goals will make it difficult to make a specific timeline or know the approximate time needed to achieve your goals.

Chapter 5

Put Your Plan on Paper

Importance of Putting Your Plan on Paper

It is important to write things down—the things that we plan on achieving that is. A study reveals that while more men did this than women, those who did were fewer than 20 percent. Writing down goals was prove to be helpful in achieving one's goals. Jotting down your plans makes things manifest in some ways. First, you are storing down the information about your goal from your brain to a piece of paper. You will take something more seriously if you have a visual representation of it.

While a visual reminder is not something you can totally miss, there is an ever deeper phenomenon at play here—encoding. This is a biological process whereby the things that we think about travel to the hypothalamus for analysis. This analysis culminates the storage of information in the long-term memory area, and some get discarded. Writing increases the chances of remembering something.

Most people do not think it is important to write down their goals and plans. They float around life, relying on the day-to-day motivation they get from a simple thought, wondering why their plans never materialized.

It serves to give you a daily reminder. Writing down your goals helps you keep the end goal in mind. Great ideas pop in and out of our minds so fast in the course of the day. We miss out on significant ideas since we do not write them down. There is an increased likelihood of accomplishing something if you have it written down on paper.

It gives you accountability. The constant reminder that is a written goal will serve as a constant reminder that you have a certain goal to achieve. You will better keep track of your progress if you have something to refer to at the end of the day. In addition to enhancing feelings of excitement, writing down your goals will also help you to analyze what is working about your plan and what isn't. This way, you are better suited to make the necessary changes and see your plan to fruition.

It attracts opportunities. As you slowly begin to see some of your plans come to life, you will realize that more opportunities may come your way. Written plans help you filter these opportunities. You will realize that without a written plan, you will constantly be tempted to veer off course before you realize that you are on the wrong track.

It increases your motivation. While most people think that the simple act of thinking about something is as good as actually doing it, nothing could be farther from the truth. Thinking about something, no matter how hard we do it, is not going to produce any positive results unless we take action on it. Focusing on a focal point increases our energy flow. It's easier to direct all our thought, energy, and time toward something if we cared enough about it to write it down. The focus on a written goal increases the value of the returns and prevents us from being thrown off my life from it.

That being said, we need to make sure that our goals are written down in a clear and precise way. Writing down vague descriptions of your plans will not help you achieve much. The study suggests that specific goals, followed by a detailed plan on how to achieve the same, are the difference between wishful thinking and effective action.

Always add a deadline to your goal. A goal without a time stamp is as good as a fail. Since you will not have figured out the deadline for your goal, the urgency to get it done will slowly dissipate. More "important" things will take up your time, and before you know it, your goals will gather dust in a corner until you stumble on it later and get disappointed. Write a deadline that is challenging enough to push you into action. Be specific and reasonable when doing this because you do not want to turn your goals into a second job that you hate but feel obliged to get done.

Set deadlines that you can work with, and get the motivation to check them off one after the other as time goes. Working toward achieving your goals should be fun to do. You will be surprised to realize that it gets easier to achieve them one by one. One act motivates the next. Always keep in mind that the second rolls in after the first are done, so the completion of one milestone will give room for the action of the second and so on. It's all about the law of attracting good vibes.

Prepare Your To-Do List before Bed

When it comes to bedtime, most of us sit on our computers, catch up on the latest gossip on social media, or watch Netflix before we doze off. While most of us may not put much consideration into the things we do before bed, you will be surprised to learn that they either make or break us. Some of the activities we indulge in, like binge-watching a series or staring at our phone screens, can affect our sleeping cycles and slowly form habits that are hard to beat later in life.

Before closing the day, highly successful people have a pre-set routine that they follow. Although having one might seem monotonous and repetitive, what most of us fail to understand is that success lies in our habits. Putting down your next-day to-do list alleviates feelings of anxiety.

If you struggle with getting the shut-eye immediately you get into bed, the most tempting habit would be taking out your phone and letting it lull you to sleep. This is considered unhealthy. Studies reveal that writing down your list for the next day enables you to sleep nine minutes faster than someone who does not. Before bed, you have an easier time to slowly wind down and close the day by mentally preparing your mind for the tasks that lie ahead.

You may not have put much thought into what you do before bed, but these simple actions can change how our night progresses and, generally, the mood we wake up in the next day. Granted, everyone has a routine they ascribe to before bed, but whether they serve you or not is something of debate for another day. Some healthy things to get into before bed are suggested here:

1. **Read a good book.** A few pages of your favorite book will put you in a clear state of mind. Reading is beneficial in the long run, and developing a reading habit enables you to learn while you are asleep as your brain processes the things you've read while you are asleep. Choose your books wisely as the material we consume might be the reason we have restless nights or a peaceful night's sleep.

2. **Meditate.** Taking time to meditate on your life gives you focus and keeps you grounded. Meditation is a proven way to relax your mind into a deep sleep naturally. Whether it is a prayer or some minutes of meditation, spending some time in silence will help you give clarity on the important areas in your life.

3. **Plan.** We like to revisit the activities that we had during the day as a measure of how successful the day was. This is a nice way to reflect on the things that we could have done differently. While it is a critical way to know where we stand, thinking back will only tie us in the past and cause us anxiety for the coming day. Besides contemplating the day that was, it is important to use this time to plan out the day ahead of us. Additionally, the previous day's activities should be able to help us make a to-do list for the next day. The best thing about this is that planning your day the night before gives you a road map on the direction you are heading and how to get there.

With time, you will find it easier to understand the things that work for you and those that do not. This is caused by building up the anticipation the night before. Of course, nobody wants to have a bad day. The thoughts that we have about our days and ourselves are positive. While there may be a thin line between pessimism and realism, focusing on the positive parts for the next day gives you a feel-good attitude in the morning. The mood that you wake up in can either make or break you. Waking up confused, unprepared, and already riled up will do nothing for your already busy day. All this can change by just adapting a small habit of taking a few minutes apart to plan what you want to achieve the following day.

Rules Are Made to Be Broken

This phrase is said because breaking rules is a virtue of creativity outside the box. It is not said in a bid to encourage immorality, which is a matter of opinion, anyway. It neither means that one should act illegally and break the law, which is subject to every individual jurisdiction. Rules are made to keep on the safer side of things. There is a certain caliber of people that go ahead to trump every rule and take risks, and they find that in doing so, they excel in their field. This explains why we loudly laud the rule breakers that progress in society and punish those who break the rules for their gain.

Steve Job challenged us to "think different." You cannot be different from everyone else if you all subscribe to the same mantra. Rules are broken by those who dare to do so and achieve their desires while those who play it safe live a normal life by trying too hard not to color outside the lines. Breaking the rules for the right reasons will catapult you to reach your destiny while following the rules set by society will only take you so far.

Case in point, there are many rules in art, music, and the creative works that tend to be broken by artists, looking for new and creative solutions to understand the world around them. Most artists are often ridiculed in their sole journey for becoming different. They are isolated by society for being daring enough to test the uncharted waters. This is usually right before their genius reveals itself to society.

Artists provoke society for centuries. Nobody that made a difference stood with the crowds. The provocations and mocking happen but only for a while. With time, as you get stubborn in your path, the society softens and even lauds you for your efforts. It is not celebrated until the difference is clearly understood. Unfortunately, fear of the unknown has and will continue to enclose people in their cocoon of mental barriers, living life with unrealized potential.

Create Your Happiness

There's a reaction to every action. This law encompasses every aspect of your life. You get what you give. You are solely responsible for the way your life is and how it will turn out. If you feel that your current situation is not very likable, the chances are that you allowed it that way.

The good news is that you have the power to change the way your life is and how you see it at any moment. With new choices and a better attitude, you can turn your life around. Finding your path can be a grueling thing. It's not easy, and it includes a lot of trial and error. The important thing to keep in mind is that the process of becoming your true self is a lifetime journey.

Nothing is set in stone. Interest, abilities, and personalities change with time. You are not the same person you were five years ago, as you will not be in a decade. This fact stresses the reason success should not be viewed as a destination but a journey.

Humans are very adaptable creatures, and as you better understand yourself, you will find it better to change your life ultimately. You must begin to prioritize yourself above other things. You need first to identify and then prioritize the things you consider most important. Here are a few things that will help you create the life you want.

Think about What You Want

Knowing what you want in life can be a challenge. However, it is not possible to live life in your terms if you don't know what it is you want. You need to prioritize your journey. That way, you know what you are working toward. Look within yourself and identify the things that make you feel alive, what matters most to you, and what makes you happy.

We often make the mistake of thinking that thinking about ourselves makes us selfish. Asking yourself what you prioritize doesn't mean that you will ignore everyone else around you. It just means that after the exercise, you will have a better understanding of how to live your life the best way you can. Conversely, identifying what you want includes recognizing the people that matter and realizing that caring for them is as big a step in making you happy as it is doing it for yourself.

Differentiate Yourself

We are all unique individuals. Much of our identity, though, comes from our initial interactions with our caretakers and the environment we live in. As a result, much of our identity is cloned from these factors and not our own. You must differentiate yourself from the person you are because of environmental influence.

Aside from environment and daily interactions, most people take up the culture and values they grew up in, or due to defiance, they rebel and act completely different from expected. However, to create your life, you need to develop your values, as opposed to following those of your influencers.

This may mean that you might encounter some negative reaction. As you start living out your life, many people will feel threatened by this and, as a result, will oppose the move. You should not view this as a barricade, rather as reinforcement that you are doing something right for you.

Stop Listening to Your Inner Critic

The journey to self-realization and actualization is riddled with setbacks. Most of these are external and quite harmless if you know how to handle them. The others are internal and could be dangerous. It's the inner voice. This is the first enemy that you are likely going to encounter. The critical inner voice is akin to a bad coach that lives in your head. It encompasses negative thoughts, attitudes, and beliefs that go against your best interests and goals.

The inner critic acts against you. It evaluates your every plan and, for each, comes up with multiple reasons as to why you will fail. This subconscious voice acts to diminish your self-esteem by attempting to keep things as they are. The critical voice realizes that change is difficult and, as a result, tries to reinforce the old lifestyle by criticizing the one you're trying to live.

Most people have developed a system that helps them tune out voices from other people. This is a great thing since you eliminate the external factors that hold you back. What we don't realize, however, is that, if left unchecked, the inner critic could do more harm than you could ever imagine. You must find a way to mute the inner critic too.

Whenever you notice your mind drifting to negative, self-deprecating thoughts, stop yourself immediately. Divert your thoughts elsewhere, maybe to the things you are happy about in your life. This way, you do not get caught up evaluating your inner critic's voice for any truths. Pay attention to what triggers the thoughts, and be sure to notice this every time. With time, you will notice a pattern to what initiates these thoughts, and will be able to handle them better next time.

Harness Your Power

As you slowly overcome your inner critic, you will cultivate more power. Personal power is a healthy form of self-assertion that reflects your natural determination to give and receive love, satisfaction, success, and meaning in your life. This is a journey based on confidence, competence, and strength from your part.

The greatest challenge and highest form of reward stem from living the life that you consciously create. You don't have to live a long life, have the fattest bank account, or travel every corner of the earth. All you have to do is craft your own life and live it.

Set Realistic Goals

Once you are in touch with what you are after in life, it is important to align your goals with this. Living your best life should be a top priority goal for you. The secret to goal setting is to keep them as simple as possible. Simple in this regard means that they should be small and attainable. The specificity of your goals has a direct effect on whether or not you will achieve them.

Since these are goals that you are setting for yourself, do not go all out writing down hard-to-hit targets just for the sake of feeling big and all important. The smaller goals are easier to relate to and effectively beat. Achieving these goals is an important part of living your life.

The actions are the hardest part. It does you no good to simply write down your goals and then fantasize about the ideal life but do nothing toward attaining that life. Although uncomfortable, getting out of your comfort zone is the best way to start.

Fill Your Day with Tiny Things You Love

Happiness is in the details. Make your day work for you. If you know that a certain person is grouchy and difficult to deal with, the best way is to avoid them, right? From the moment you leave the bed until you get back in, you should plan your day in such a way that you inadvertently introduce small but significant things that are likely to brighten your day.

Even though you might encounter unavoidable situations that might spin your day out of control, you will ultimately have the power in your hands. Going about your day allowing your mood to be set by external factors and people is a sure way to fail.

Do Something New

You can always renew your energy levels by trying something new every once in a while. Routines are limiting and get boring with time. Trying a new recipe, hairstyle, or workout technique could be all you need to rejuvenate your body and spirit into your new lifestyle. New things not only keep us young but also remind us that life is so full of great things that we haven't tried out yet. As the new psyche catches on, you will realize your energy levels and courage multiply.

Chapter 6

Healthy Living

Choosing the Right Diet

Is there a best diet? What do you consider a good diet? The truth is, no diet plan works for everyone. Every single person has unique needs from the next person. This only goes to stress that because of this, your diets may not be the same. The best diet plan is the one that is fashioned explicitly for you and is designed for the long term. Short-term and sporadic diets are not only unhealthy, but they throw our minds and bodies into a state of confusion.

A diet is what a person eats or drinks. Essentially, it encompasses much more than just the food and drinks part. It has more to do with your general lifestyle and the things that you involve yourself in day after day. Different types of diets are taken up by people for different reasons. Some are fashioned to lose weight, others to gain muscle, and yet some are designed to attain a healthy mind and body.

Many marketing claims glorify one diet over another, and this may make it hard for you to sort through which ones work and which one is a fad. The trick is to go through this with a long-term mentality. A "lose weight fast" diet may succeed in enabling you to lose some pounds in a few months. The question is "What next?" Most of these diets are not sustainable, and as a result, they do more harm than good.

Diets should be viewed as personal plans for your body and mind. No two people are alike. This mentality will enable you to critically look at a few aspects of your life that will allow you to create a working diet for yourself.

Look at Your Lifestyle

Before you embark on a diet, you need to think about the lifestyle that you currently lead critically. Look at the number of hours that you have every week to prepare your meals, work out, and relax personally. Do you travel a lot? Do you work from your home office? Do you eat out more than you do at home?

These questions should help you create a diet that will fit your current schedule. The point of a diet is not to disrupt your routine and throw your course. A diet needs to consider changing as little of your life as possible. Otherwise, you may plunge your body into stress.

Look at the things that you are willing to change and adapt to incorporate a healthy diet. These changes should be for good. Consider making a few more home-cooked meals or taking an evening stroll right after you eat and before stretching. These activities shouldn't take more than two hours of your evening that might have otherwise been spent seated in front of the television.

Study Your Eating Habits

Since your diet will mostly revolve around the things that you eat, you need to study the way that you eat at the moment. If your eating habits involve eating out more at restaurants or ordering home deliveries, it may be a stretch to create a plan that involves complex recipes and an all home-cooked plan.

You are your habits. Maybe the way you eat is fashioned around the most practical method for you. Either way, creating a diet synonymous with your current eating plans have the highest rate of success. Consider your dietary preference to ensure that you have a plan that keeps you well fed and healthy throughout the day.

Know Your Nutritional Needs

Many diet plans promise immediate results. These are the ones that most usually come with a cost that we either ignore or don't notice. You need to know what your nutritional needs are. A waitress who spends most of her day on her feet will have different nutritional needs from an accountant who spends her day balancing books at her desk.

The best diets meet your nutritional needs. Anything that will have drastic changes while compromising on nutritional needs often does not last. If you cannot identify your nutritional needs by yourself, get the help of a dietician. He or she will use your age, lifestyle, activity levels, health history, and environment to fashion a diet that will have lasting positive effects.

Define Your Diet Goals and Expectations

Your diet plan should heavily depend on the goals and expectations that you have set for yourself. A healthy body gives rises to a healthy mind. Most people who set goals for their lives come to realize that part of this usually requires that they adopt a healthier diet and lifestyle. You need to be clear with yourself on what you need your diet to do for you.

Are you trying to lose weight, be more active, or add some natural protein into your diet? Why are you trying to do this? If you aren't sure where to start, ask yourself why you are getting on a diet, and be relentless with your answers until you get one that truly goes into the heart of the matter.

Consider setting small attainable goals that are easier to beat as opposed to grand schemes that are attractive but near impossible. If you don't enjoy your diet, mentally and physically, you need to review it. This is because, at the end of the day, the point is not to punish you but to push you into the unrealized potential that you possess. Setting and hitting smaller goals will keep you motivated to conquer your larger ones.

What's Your Budget?

One other thing to consider when revising your budget is the percentage of your financials that you can comfortably set aside for your diet. Since following a diet will most likely involve a few changes in your life, it goes without saying that you will most likely have to adjust your budget accordingly.

Restocking your pantry or getting yourself workout clothes come with a price. You need to be able to consciously look at the budget that you operate with and make the necessary adjustments. Estimate your weekly or monthly spending and see if the diet you choose is sustainable. If the need arises, explore cheaper versions of the things that you need to minimize the budget but still get results.

By choosing a diet that suits your nutritional plans, lifestyle, and budget, you will well be on your way to meeting your goals. You need to balance these aspects of your life carefully for maximum results.

Work Out

Do you have a workout plan? Do you own it? Like your diet, your workout plan should be carefully tailored to cater to your lifestyle. Sure, your best friend loves cardio and weights, but that doesn't mean that the same routine would work wonders for you too. It is essential to find a routine that enables you to maintain strength and flexibility.

Exercise has many advantages. It boosts your energy levels, enhances better circulation, rids the body of toxins, and gives you a great and vibrant aura. Do not get a workout plan that includes a weight-loss regime. This is the common misconception that many people operate on. They believe in workout only as a means to fix a problem they have with their bodies.

The truth about working out could not be farther from reality on the ground. You should work out because you love your body, not because you hate it. There are many reasons to work out; let's look at a few:

1. It Boosts Immunity

Having a regular workout schedule can do more for your body than vitamins and prescription medication ever will. Studies show that the people who regularly exercise have lower chances of developing certain diseases, like diabetes, heart complications, flu, and some cancers.

Smart, goal-oriented people tend to use the workout as prevention to many ailments that afflict their counterparts. It's honestly the smartest way to operate. Instead of sitting on bad habits and having to be forced by a doctor to put in the regular jog, how about creating a habit of enjoying it by yourself and preventing a situation where you have to do it to survive?

More often than not, we tend to ignore the importance that sleep has in our day-to-day schedules. Lack of sleep shortens our life spans, elevates stress levels, depletes our attention spans, and make us irritable. You will probably find yourself losing sleep because of the looming work ahead of you tomorrow or unaccomplished tasks and goals. An overall feeling of restlessness can keep you awake long after the lights go off.

Your workout essentially tires out your body. As you work out, you release the tension on your mind and body. The body is known to carry stress in some parts, like the neck, shoulders, back, and legs. Going to bed with an aching body due to the complexities of life is not a good idea. You will wake up feeling even worse the next day, and you might experience burn out at the course of the week.

Many of our friends have had to take a day off or two because of mental and physical fatigue. All this can be curbed by doing regular workouts. Not only does it distress our minds, but it also works our bodies to build flexibility and resilience. A person who works out is better suited at handling a grueling day than one who doesn't. Working out gets you tired at the end of the session and sends you to sleep much easier and faster. You will most likely have a full night's sleep and wake up feeling more energetic and stronger.

2. It Gives You a Creative Boost

Many high-achieving people, from tech billionaires to notable artists, swear by the regular workout. We have heard more than once how an author used workout and change of scenery to beat writer's block.

Have many problems are you encountering that just seems impossible? Are you lacking inspiration and don't know where to begin? Consistent exercise can enhance your cognitive abilities. It is an inexpensive way to get your mental faculties moving and is additionally super healthy. A study revealed that being physically active proved to increase the ability to think creatively and flexible. This was true only if the person in question were used to being active and remained that way.

Exercise helps you improve your ability to focus your attention on a particular task. If you find yourself with wandering thoughts that prevent you from paying attention to one thing, the chances are that exercise could solve this problem for you. It helps combat stress and depression by increasing the production of serotine, which is depleted by anxiety and depression. Physical activity stimulates the growth of new brain cells in the hippocampus, essentially improving your memory.

Working out makes you feel good about your body, and when you feel good, you look great. As a result, you attract good things to you. It's a chain reaction. There is no better way to get the creative juices flowing than with a good workout session.

3. It Increases Self-Confidence

Are you feeling down lately? Do you feel like things just don't seem to be going the way you had envisioned? This is a familiar feeling that many people get once in a while. We all need a confidence boost, but more often than not, we don't get it. Confidence is long-lasting as long as it comes from within you. All the praise in the world will do nothing for you if you do not already feel good about yourself.

You are limitless if you are confident. Working out brings out your confidence. With the advent of the internet and social media, so much emphasis is put on physical appearance. We are focused on the outside appearance of people and things now more than ever. This is not necessarily a negative thing.

Working out builds your body to be the best medium for your life journey. It gives you a beautiful body. You feel better about yourself, and as a result, the attraction reflects on other people. People will get drawn to you because of how you look, whether you like it or not. If you incorporate a workout schedule for yourself, you never have to worry about what you look like on the outside because consistency and putting in the work will do wonders for you.

Chapter 7

Proven Strategies on How Effective Time Management Simplifies Your Life

Time Management

Time management is all about effectively spending every minute of your time with the aim of accomplishing your goals. Although time management could sound like a simple subject, the practice itself is a difficult exercise. It involves a lot of balancing between social life, work, and hobbies. You need to balance all these acts according to priorities. Unlike the past, most people prefer to deal with the most unpleasant task before tackling those tasks that are relatively easy to deal with.

Without a proper time management strategy, you will end up spending your time on frenzy activities, and at the end of the day, you will end up beating yourself, wondering how you have been able to accomplish less than you anticipated. The only way to increase your productivity is to stay cool, collected, and disciplined to your time management formula.

The subject of time is relative to everyone. Everyone is subjected to aging mortality. It is your responsibility to utilize time well. A time that passes can never be retrieved. Tomorrow can never be a replica of today. Activities that are performed on time will likely be productive or fruitful.

Tips for an Effective Time Management System

Take a Moment to Plan and Organize Time

There is a perception out there that sitting down and planning how you will spend your time is a waste of time. Although this may sound a cliché, I should remind you that failing to plan is equivalent to planning to fail. The best thing that will help you here is your diary and calendar. It is time to forget the "should" and "will" mentality.

Prioritize Well

Vilfredo, an Italian economist, invented the 80–20 rule. He noted that 20 percent effort leads to 80 percent reward. When using this rule, it is important to identify those efforts with the greatest rewards. Start with them before going for those efforts with list rewards. Once you have identified those efforts, use color, numbers, or letters to prioritize them. Another important factor when prioritizing activities is sorting out tasks with datelines. Indicate the dateline somewhere. If possible, set the alarm as a reminder for the dateline.

To-Do List

This is a list of your day-to-day activities. Some people cannot work without a to-do list. The day-to-day activities are put in a calendar to serve as a reminder and others written down. Some will constantly be changed while others cannot be altered.

Go for a method that you feel suits you best. Do not be afraid of trying several methods before settling on one method that suits you best.

Flexibility Is Key

Time management experts have suggested that it is important to plan for 50 percent of your time to distractions and flexibility. In your day-to-day activities, you will have emergencies once in a while. It is, therefore, important to consider these unexpected happenings when planning for your day. It is important to note that not all interruptions are worth giving our time. Alter your time only for important and unavoidable interruptions.

What Time Are You Most Productive

It is not true that everyone is most productive in the morning. Some people are most productive during the night while others in the wee hours of the day. No one knows your prime hours except yourself. Set the most difficult task to the time of the day when you are most active. Then set the simplest task to a time when your body is mostly inactive. Most people experience this moment in the afternoon. Through this method, be assured of an increase in your productivity.

Do Not Try to Be a Perfectionist

Most people fail in life while trying to be too perfect in whatever they are doing. Much as it is good to pay attention to every detail of whatever you are doing, putting too much time to this may lead to perfectionism. This is the act of repeating yourself too much in an effort of being perfect. There is a belief in the Malaysian culture the only perfectionist in the world is a god.

Learn to Say No

Difficult situations make or break a man. Sometime you are faced with unscheduled activities touching on your family or friends. Depending on the urgency of these activities, you have to be strong enough to reject them. Beware that your decision may not go well with others. Take your time to explain the reason for your decision and what completing whatever you were doing meant to you.

Planning Ahead

One of the best decisions you can ever do in life is planning. This requires a lot of discipline. It is the best way to maximize your effectiveness in what you are doing. You will be able to anticipate the happenings of the future. When planning, here are a few things you need to consider:

- What are your goals?

- What are the timelines for achieving your goals?

- What software part of me do I need to achieve my goal (i.e., knowledge, information, or skills)?

- Do I have the necessary materials that will enable me to achieve my goals?

- Can I accomplish my goals on my own or with the assistance of others?

- Are my goals achievable?

Without setting the above question, you will find yourself failing. You are likely to decide the path of your life when it is too late. Through this, you might lose hope since time will not be on your side. Also, without a clear path, you will end up stooping too low, hence underachieving.

Reason Planning Ahead Is Important

1. It Helps in Assessing Future Risks and Opportunities

To achieve success in life, you must be able to take risks. Risks remove you from the comfort zone. Through planning, you will be to take paths that others fear taking with confidence. In the case of improper planning, however, the uncalculated risk could lead to massive losses.

Plans help us weigh the possible risk. Categorize them before planning on how to mitigate these risks in case they do not go as expected. Many people fail because they fail to anticipate the risks or fail to plan for these anticipated risks.

2. Planning Helps You Become Proactive

Through planning, you will be able to act right on anticipated challenges. You will be able to respond to situations instead of reacting to them. You will be able to allocate enough time and resources since you anticipated the problem.

3. Planning Improves Your Performance

Researchers have established a direct correlation between planning and execution. A well-thought plan leads to good performance. It is natural that when it is clear what you are doing next, you will be less anxious, which creates a good working environment at work.

4. You Will Have Adequate Time to Develop Your Team

In the increasingly competitive business world, without a good team to help you in achieving your dreams, you will fail. Planning will enable you to assign the right job to the right person. Can you imagine a situation where an emergency hits you at your workplace? You will end up assigning jobs to different people randomly. Through this, you are likely to fail terribly. If you had planned ahead, however, your team would be ready to tackle any job that is given to them according to their strength and liking.

Key Routine Habits That Will Help Simplify Your Life

Simplifying your life is a philosophy in life that is workable if done in the right manner. First, you should understand that time is a sacred thing that should be used strategically. To utilize time factor well to achieve your goals, do not let the unnecessary things to distract you. Through an organized life, you will have more free time, less stress, and less anxiety.

It is not boring at all to live an organized life. It is all about taking the basics with the seriousness it deserves. Do not waste your time on things that do not matter or add any value to your life. Through time management, consider the following to organize and simplify your life:

Create a Routine

This a structure of how your day-to-day activities will go about. A clear day-to-day structure eliminates stress and anxiety. Can you imagine walking every day to work but not being sure what it is all about? Your routine should start in the morning; plan your mealtime, laundry, and any other day-to-day activity. A routine also helps you not to forget or miss any important activity in your life.

Automate Activities That You Can

Bills, such as house rent, taxes, power bill, and other subscriptions, should be automated. Trust me, this will save a lot of your time. The nature of reoccurrence makes these activities boring. Many times, my TV subscriptions have been cut following my failure to make payments on time. This happened to me until I set an automated payment. Money is deducted directly from my account, and I love it!

Track All Your Expenses

There is a perception out there that only the broke will always look into their expenses. It is not true. Find time to read a book on Bill Gates's lifestyle. Write down all your expense at the moment you spend money. Audit all your expenditure. At times, you blame people for stealing your money, yet you have used it to buy something. Also, this will help in improving how you spend your cash. Do not be that person who goes to the bar with your monthly income and comes out with nothing.

A Daily Essential Kit

Are you that person who carries almost all your belongings on your shoulder every day? It is time to quit that lifestyle. Get a mini daily essential kit and pack things that you need for that day. For instance, my daily kit will have car keys, painkiller, a laptop, and a bottle of water. I may need other things, but they are not essential; I can do without them.

Quit Multitasking

Research has shown that this cannot work. Nobody can effectively shift their focus on different things effectively. This is notorious for men. Compared to men, women can multitask better. This is not a good practice. Put all your uninterrupted attention on one thing before moving to another. The brain of a human being was designed to do one thing at a go. If you are used to doing several activities at a go, try single tasking and see the results. You will be amazed.

Always Go for Quality over Quantity

Do less and do it better. Never compromise quality to saving money. This will eliminate a lot of clutter in your life. Quality also gives much-needed satisfaction, hence reducing the stress after a bad decision. Focus on the things you love, and that can stay for long.

Start Batching Things

It is all about classifying your tasks. Take for instance reading and replying your e-mails. Dedicate thirty minutes of your time a day to go through your mail. How many meetings do you hold in a day? If more than one, it is time you relook at your program. Hold one meeting, either in the morning or in the evening. Another activity that consumes a lot of time is receiving and making phone calls. Unless it is a work-related phone call, do not take calls at work. It leads to distractions.

Follow the Two-Minute Rule

It is a simple rule. Everything that can be done in less than two minutes should be done with immediate effect. Did you know that it is the small things that complicate things in your life? Completing these small tasks will make your mind ready for the important things.

Learn to Celebrate Your Accomplishments

There is no doubt that at the end of every season or year, there is something to celebrate about yourself. It is often easy to point out areas that you have underachieved, hence forgetting what we achieved. To pay tribute to these achievements, look back at your goals. Point out those that you achieved; it uplifts your spirit. Point to note, however, is that do not look down upon those goals that you failed to achieve. As you celebrate, think of ways to improve and achieve more in the coming season.

To help you in pinpointing these achievements, write down at least ten things you have achieved in the past year. As you do that, look at how each accomplishment has changed your life. Discuss with your spouse each of your successes. This might change the perception of how your spouse views you. At times, our spouses think we are not doing enough to improve the situation of our families. It is, therefore, important to celebrate your achievements with them.

Celebrating your accomplishments actually sets the ground for setting the next goals. Also, when you are aware of your accomplishments, you will be able to set goals that surpass your previous goals.

Set Small and Big Goals

If your goal is getting 10 million dollars in fifteen years, break down your goals into five years, then one year respectively. This will help you gauge whether you are on the right track or not. Also, you will be able to celebrate your achievements in bits. I mean you will not wait for fifteen years to celebrate your goals. Life is too short!

Celebrate an Achievement That Comes Your Way

Whenever you reach a milestone on your journey to achieving your goals, sit back and celebrate. The days off that your company gives after an achievement feel so nice! Acknowledging employees' achievements boosts their morale. They will want to achieve more and more.

Take a Moment to Brag!

I know this does not sound good to you; it is good to brag about your achievements. Do not lock yourself in a room and celebrate. Call a press conference if possible. Invite your college alumni or even write an article highlighting what you have been able to do. This will probably change the public perception about you, hence raising your profile, which is nice. It raises your self-esteem.

Think about Your Humble Beginning

Many times, you feel you have not achieved much, which is not the case. If you take a moment to look at where you are now and where you were five years ago, you will realize how much you have achieved. Yes, you might not be where you want to be, but you have achieved so much since the inception of your company or business.

Feel Lucky

Yes, you are fortunate to be where you are today. I had two college mates, and we all shared the same dreams of starting our own companies. Unfortunately, one of them got into an accident and was paralyzed; the other is battling with stage 4 cancer. Looking at this unfortunate circumstance that befell my friends, I ask myself, "Why should I not feel lucky?" If you can wake up every day to go to work, your family is well, you are healthy, then you have a reason to celebrate.

Do Not Expect to Achieve All Your Dreams

The most successful people in this world have unfulfilled dreams. Billionaires, presidents, entrepreneurs all wish they had more time in life. All these people have something they would have wanted to achieve in their lifetime. You are not any different; you will never achieve all your goals. Celebrate what you have been able to accomplish.

Think Big

Your career will come to an end someday. Have you ever taken some time to think about your life after your career? Many times, you find yourself destroying some bridges in an effort of building others. Do not neglect your family in making your career. It is high time you start balancing your life, much as you need to achieve your goals, you also need your friends and family. Carry them through your journey of success, celebrate your achievements with them, and above all, appreciate their efforts in helping you shape your life.

Chapter 8

The Power of Belief

The strength of belief is one of the significant factors that culminate reality. To create your reality, you must be able to believe that you already have that which you desire. Belief in oneself is the reason behind the highest performance levels. High belief motivates you to perform better and more effectively; it's the driving force. This is true in athletics, business, personal relationships, education, etc.

Belief can either empower you or limit you. In the presence of belief, your performance soars while the absence of which results in reduced performance. The good thing is that you have a choice to either believe in yourself or not. It's entirely up to you. No one can instill belief in you without your permission. First, there has been a seed already growing inside you. It's a given; you must be able to believe in yourself to see any tangible result.

Why Belief Is So Strong

The power of belief lies in your ability to do four things. Belief creates strength of will, vision, and resilience. It ignites your creativity. Belief creates into reality the invisible reality that only you can create in your mind. You are limited only to your thoughts, and as a result, you must put in the work to reach your goals. All the belief in yourself will result in nothing if you do not have a fighting spirit. In as much as belief happens in mind, you must have both the mental and physical stamina to follow through. Otherwise, you will live in a make-believe world.

The path that you take in life, the one that will eventually lead you into creating your reality, has to be identified with exceptional clarity.

There must not be room for feeling your way in the dark. You need to have a way to achieve your goals, and that is mainly what the path is all about. If your reality requires that you train relentlessly, study hard, or practice day and night, this is what you must do. You must be able to ignore any distraction that may cloud your path, ignore anyone that does not fit into your plan, and focus all your energy on the path that you have chosen.

Granted, you will come across many obstacles, most of which will either be physical or mental ones. Case in point, you believe you will finish in the top three of a ten-kilometer run. You must practice hard beforehand. Physical work is not easy. The work will drain your energy levels. You will develop blisters, sore muscles, and occasional cramps. You will feel like giving up. You might start hearing a voice in your mind telling that top ten is just as good as top three.

In addition to your own body trying to stop you, you will get ridiculed by the people around you. The biggest problem is that usually those that know us are our biggest stumbling block. Ridicule and criticism are things that you will come to know on a personal level. You must connect with your mind and essentially block out anything else that might distract you.

The strength of will takes you through the hard days. It is not just about starting. It involves the strength to sustain yourself and remain positive even when the journey gets difficult. Under pressure, people rise to the level of the training they have. Challenging situations put pressure on your mind. Winning first in your mind will help you sustain your body through the journey to achieving your goals. You have to be fully present mentally. Talent and physical training are not enough to get you to your end goal. Mental strength plays just a huge part as any.

Belief ignites the creativity in you. It unleashes your potential. Since belief has no excuses whatsoever, it unleashes in you the focus you require to access your full capabilities. It is true; we are not aware of what we are truly capable of. Believing first that we can do it and then going on ahead to work for it brings out our inner capabilities.

Give Your Belief a Name

The power of words and conviction is something that we mostly ignore. Language is a vehicle in which our convictions materialize. The limitations to what you can achieve are contained in what you know. The words that we speak or the thoughts that we entertain (although left unsaid) have the power to either make or break our spirit.

The first step to believing in something is to simply have the disposition to validate that belief. Reality is built on a collective on beliefs, starting from the most personal and intimate ones and spanning into the group beliefs, country-wide beliefs, and finally, world beliefs. The validation of your dreams makes you trust in them. As a result, you will trust the process and get the commitment to support your belief.

You have to understand that belief is not only about individual performance. It is about collective effort. An elite team that believes in each other and their collective mission can reach a level of elite performance. Shared belief creates clarity and team effort.

Consider yourself a champion and then treat and act like one. Talking to oneself with positive reinforcement should go a long way in validating your dreams. Like mentioned earlier, there is immense power in the words that we hear and even more in the things that we tell ourselves. Nobody will believe in us if we don't believe in ourselves first.

Dance to the Beat of Your Drum

We are brought into this world with the primary knowledge of who we are. We usually already know what we want to experience in the world. There is a drum beating in our souls meant to guide us toward the path that will get us to our desired results. To be happy, always dance to the tune of your drum.

Christopher Morley believed that the only success in life is to be able to live life the way you believe. Look at your life. Are you living it as you want, or are you dancing to the tune that others have made for you?

The truth is that success is a very personal journey. The success that you name for yourself is the goal that once achieved will make you and only you happy. Success on any other person's terms is not true success. It might be so for the other person, but it will not be so for us. This is the reason is why having money does not equate happiness. It can lead to destruction if mishandled.

To achieve success, you must first define what success means to you. You must define it on a very personal level, and then and only then can you truly focus on it. Living a life that is not yours leads to an unhappy life. Living on someone else's terms will get you looking back and wondering what you had been working toward. This loss in direction will depress you over time, giving you feelings of uselessness and fatigue.

Being comfortable in your skin means being happy to let others see you for who you are. It means being open about your vulnerabilities and failure, being human enough to admit when we need help and when it's time to stop. You must understand that a heightened sense of self is not the same as confidence. That just breeds arrogance and is repulsive.

Eliminating the conflict between who you are as an individual and at work is fulfilling. This brings out your knowledge in yourself, and ultimately, every decision you make will be in line with your values. The good news is that, with the internet and the global market, you can get enough money in any field to live comfortably. This means that you may as well do it in a manner that reflects your true values and matches your personality. The most dangerous thing is following the tide with everyone else. If you can earn well enough to support yourself comfortably, why would you want to live any other way?

You can easily design a business model around yourself. This is vital to the success of your business. Piggybacking on someone else's ideas will not take you far. It will have you working tirelessly to build someone else's dream as opposed to your own. There is no shortcut here. There is no one-size-fits-all approach to this. To achieve success in your endeavor, you have to work on a model that maximizes your strengths and minimizes your weaknesses. These are unique to every single one of us as a business model is also unique to each of us.

It is hard to achieve success in business if it is not built on your blueprint. You must imprint your impression on it for it to work. Running with the pack may give you company but will not satisfy you. It is not fulfilling to do what is expected of you by others. In as much as you might do the job well, it will feel like you are wearing an ill-fitting suit. Although the suit might cover you and prevent cold, it will never feel right. Have you ever had a negative feeling about something and it doesn't go away until you do something about it? Well, that's your premonition talking to you. Most of us ignore these feelings, but the problem is that it doesn't go away until it has been identified and acted on. Imagine living your whole life trying to silence this feeling. At the end of the journey, you will have just one question to answer: "Was it all worth it?" Most of the time, the answer is a painful no. Ask yourself the following questions:

- Does my life make any sense?

- Would I keep this job if I didn't need the money?

- Is this the best version of myself?

- Am I moving in the right direction?

- Am I living the best version of myself?

If the answers you have for these questions don't satisfy you, then it's time to make some changes. Align your thought, strength, and energy in your direction.

Finding Your Inspiration

Who Is a Role Model?

A role model is an individual whom you revere and look up to. Admiration of your role model aids you in determining the right behaviors to adopt. A role model is an individual whom you aspire to be like, whether in the future or the present. He or she might be a person you know and even interact with daily or someone you have met once. Role models can either be negative or positive. Negative role models serve as examples of disruptive and harmful mannerisms while positive role models set a good example of positive behaviors.

Anyone can be a role model. Those who embrace the Western way of life select public figures as their role models, such as actors, athletes, musicians, and political officials. These people's behaviors determine whether they will be regarded as either negative or positive role models. People like drug dealers and members of gangs that perpetrate crimes are exclusively considered negative role models, owing to the ill behaviors they display.

Visibility plays a major role in making one a role model. The most conspicuous figures, such as actors and athletes, have public visibility as part of their job. Because millions of people can observe these individuals' mannerisms and way of life, it is highly probable that people will try to imitate their mannerisms and lifestyle. Even though people of all age groups have their role models, generally, it is the young people who mostly attempt to imitate their role models since they are still developing their identities.

Choosing the Right Role Model

Role models are important as they serve as a rough guide to your life and aspirations. They assist you to become the person you desire to be and also inspire you to make a difference. It is for these reasons that you ought to choose your role model wisely. Your role model will influence you positively and empower you to be the best version of yourself. Selecting a role model in your personal life is very distinct from selecting a celebrity role model.

Choosing a Role Model for Your Personal Life

How do you choose the appropriate role model for your personal life? It is advisable that you choose a role model that you know. Such a role model will assist you to mature and grow as a person. The role model can also offer you advice, guidance, as well as real-life instances of how to achieve the best in life. In choosing a role model for your personal life, also consider the negative aspects of your personality as well as your bad habits—these comprise the things you dislike or those you desire to change about yourself. These things are key in determining the person you want to become. Before choosing your role model, make a list of the key things you desire to achieve. Do you desire to live your life in a particular way? To achieve certain things? List what you want to attain, both personally and generally.

Also, ensure that you boost your confidence. As you begin to consider how to choose a role model, make an attempt of believing in yourself as an individual. The main purpose of selecting a role model is to motivate you to become a better version of yourself. It is for this reason that you should have confidence in yourself and your capabilities to become whatever kind of person you desire.

Furthermore, identify with those people that exhibit similar qualities to those that you wish to attain. If you desire to become an inspirational person, then think about the individuals that inspire you. Brainstorm on the issue and ask yourself questions like "Why do you admire them that much?" and "What message do they send to you through their actions?" Keep in mind that some great role models may be existing around you and may have a greater impact on you. They may also mentor you; hence, they serve as potential choices for your role model. When choosing a role model for your personal life, it is advisable that you go for that person that has a sense of purpose. A perfect role model is one who knows who they are. You would not want a person who seems perfect from the outside yet have no sense of purpose. Someone who does not pretend to be someone they are not is the most suitable.

For a role model in your personal life, select an individual that makes you feel good about being you. Your role model ought to be someone who considers being unique right no matter the ridicule you receive from others. They should make you develop a positive attitude toward yourself and make you feel good in your skin. One of the purposes of having a role model is to inspire and encourage you to make improvements on yourself. So if yours does not make you feel this way, then it is for the best interest for your mental well-being to choose another.

It is also advisable to choose a person who is different from you. More often than not, you are tempted to select a role model because you see some of your aspects in them. Such role models only end up holding you back because you do not alter any of your characteristics; you only perfect characteristics that already exist. Go for a role model whom you see something they have that you need to adopt because you don't have it. For instance, if you are spontaneous and bold, select a person who is known for thorough analysis and is steady.

Also, choose someone that you know; their success should resonate with your beliefs and moral values. Choose a role model that leads a healthy lifestyle and one that you admire in all aspects of their lives. Consider qualities like the ability to inspire, passion, moral values, selflessness, commitment to the community, as well as the ability to overcome obstacles. Do not also replicate your role model's mannerisms completely. Every human is prone to error, your role model included. Your role models only act as a guide and not objects of complete imitation. So make sure that you do not adopt their behaviors blindly.

Choosing a Celebrity Role Model

What do you consider precisely when choosing a celebrity role model? One, choose a celebrity who excels in a certain area that you desire to emulate. You will know about this through the media rather than personally observing them. Two, identify celebrities who have performed acts you consider admirable. This may include individuals who have contributed in charity, saved lives, assisted the needy, or even established cure to a certain disease.

Moreover, bear in mind that only deities are considered perfect. Do not expect a role model to be perfect; they are also human, hence prone to making mistakes. You can even choose a role model who is a celebrity without really emulating their personal life. This is crucial when choosing celebrity role models, particularly for your children, because most of the celebrities live personal lives that you wouldn't want your kids emulating.

Also, look for a person who lives their life similar to how you would like to live yours. If you desire to be a popular author, you should select a role model who is successful at writing. Do not copy your role model completely too. Your celebrity role model should only serve as a guide. Strive to develop your style as well. As much as it is good to emulate your role model, it is also crucial that you preserve your individuality. Adopt only those characteristics that you would like to improve about yourself and retain the rest.

Using Your Role Model to Organize and Simplify Your Life

Although some people may contend that having a role model is not necessary, you could utilize your role models to help you organize and simplify your life. Your choice of a role model may affect your career choice and opportunities. This provides a sense of direction since you set your mind toward achieving a particular thing and you also establish what you want in life, hence simplifying things for you. Role models mainly show key effects on female students since they gain confidence to pursue careers in technology, engineering, and science, which are conventionally known to be for the male gender.

Some people have their parents as their role models; their parents have a significant influence on their education, choice of careers, as well as self-efficacy. Having a role model helps you to be more organized, and it simplifies your life since you do not struggle to search for what you want. Also, by emulating the good mannerisms of your role model, you'll make more logical decisions and become organized, and you will realize that you can achieve more.

Importance of Having a Role Model

Having a role model in your life is important, but guess what is more important than that—having a *good* role model is. This is because they have an influence on what you do and the person you become eventually. Having a positive role model is key since they influence both your actions and mannerisms and motivate you to uncover your true potentials as well as overcome your weaknesses.

Although having a role model means looking up to someone else and emulating them, the ultimate goal is to be the greatest version of yourself. Having a person to emulate serves as a guide of the values to adopt; however, at the end of the day, you will always be yourself. Learning from your role model's qualities and using them to improve your existing character as well as personality may even make you someone else's role mode someday.

By having a role model, you also learn how to overcome obstacles. Every person experiences problems they have to deal with in one way or another. The moment you realize that your role model experiences problems that at first appeared insurmountable but does not let them define them or barricade them from being successful, it motivates you and helps you prepare to deal with drawbacks that you may face in the future. It is, however, not necessary that you have direct contact with your role model. All you require to learn of their obstacles and how they surmounted them is by studying them, reflecting on what they have done to achieve success. Whenever you think of them, your spirits will automatically be lifted, and you will be able to get past your difficulties.

Another importance of having a role model is that you have someone to inspire you. Whenever you lack the motivation to perform a certain task, a role model comes in handy. The moment you think about what they have achieved in life, you feel inspired to work as hard as they did to achieve whatever you desire. Furthermore, looking up to an individual who has made a significant change in the world encourages you to strive to attain the same. If you know your role model and have had regular direct contact with them, they could also mentor you, hence give you a sense of direction in your life.

Having a role model is also key since you get to learn as well as study about someone who has achieved some of the things you are passionate about. Your role model serves as a perfect subject to learn from as well as explore. Here are some of the questions you would want to explore include:

- How did they gain interest in the talent or skill they are good at?

- How long have they been performing a particular activity?

- Is there any chance that they share tips or at least hints about how to excel at that specific activity that you are also interested in?

Through getting answers to the preceding questions, you will get significant insights that you can as well apply to your personal life. If you have a celebrity model, then the internet would be a suitable source for such information.

Chapter 9

Expected Challenges
in Your Mission

In order for you to grow as an individual, challenges are paramount. They are part of life; you cannot do without challenges. They help us in improving our skills, hence making you a better person. Stephen R. Covey in one of his philosophies compares life to a gym. For you to develop muscle, you have to lift the weight. Just like the gym, you have to overcome the challenges of life to succeed.

In a difficult situation in life, here are four simple steps that will help you solve your problems.

Understand the Problem Clearly

The first step to solving your problem is understanding the problem. There is no way of solving a question you do not understand. What is that cause of your problem? Are you the main cause of the problem? Was there a way of preventing the problem from happening? Once to find answers to these fundamental questions, tackling your problem will be an easy task. If you start solving your problem without understanding it, you will find yourself solving the wrong problems.

Identify Your Strengths and the Available Resources

What are you strengths and resources that can help you in solving a problem? Did you know that you can use your strengths in solving your problem? Make a list of all the resources you need to solve your problem. Categorize them in terms of materials, skills or knowledge required, and people who can help.

1. **Materials.** These will depend on the kind of problems you are solving. You might need a computer, money, blogs, books, etc. First, utilize the materials you have. If you are short of materials, save money for a while. Use the money to purchase whatever you need. In all these processes, be focused and aggressive.

2. **Skills and strengths.** Do you trust that your skills can help you tackle your problem? Here you need to be innovative and creative. You need to understand that you are the first person that can help yourself succeed.

3. **Friends and the outside world.** You are not superhuman. Some things are just beyond you. As much as you should trust in your abilities and not over depend on others, you need to seek help whenever you are overwhelmed by something. When you feel your friend or family member is better equipped to deal with your problem, do not hesitate to let them know. If you want to learn how to keep people around you happy, I would recommend a book by Dale Carnegie with the title *How to Win Friends and Influence People*. The book is all about making those around you happy.

Design a Well-Thought Strategy

Every situation requires different strategies to deal with. The only thing that is constant is the determination of dealing with the situation. After analyzing your problem and assembling everything needed to solve the problem, it is time to start executing it effectively. Always be flexible. In case you execute your strategy effectively without success, think of changing your strategy.

Implement Your Plan as Efficiently as Possible

Here you need all your effort, hard work, and intelligence. In every step you take, make the wisest choices. Bear in mind that one wrong move could ruin everything that you have worked so hard for. Your strategy could, however, fail terribly. Here are the possible reasons why your strategy could fail.

1. **You could have chosen a strategy that is not viable.** Relook at your plan; you should either improve it or change it, depending on your analysis. In case you have to change your strategy totally, seek advice from people who have probably been through the same problem. Learn about their experience and how they were able to deal with it effectively.

2. **You could have failed in the process of implementation.** This happens a lot. Despite having an effective well-designed strategy, you fail to implement your plan well. One poor decision during the implementation stage could ruin everything. Think about how hard you have worked to reach where you are.

Pain and Failure Are Life's Greatest Teachers

Nobody loves to fail or suffer. As an entrepreneur, I have come to learn that the failures of my past are the ones responsible for my current success. A healthy approach of life is learning through your failures. However, constant failure could ruin your career, especially if you are not the boss. Nobody will allow you to learn from their companies.

Failure is not caused by one decision but rather a series of small choices you regularly make without putting much thought into it. If you go back and scrutinize all those decisions, you will find where you went wrong. If the mistake was not in the strategy but in the wrong decisions you made, learn from your mistakes and solve the problem. If the mistake was on the strategy, change it and find other ways of dealing with the problem.

Make the Greatest Out of Your Worst Moments

No matter how successful you may be, you have had the worst moment at one point in your life. These moments happen in all parts of our lives, from family, work, school, or any other event of life. When hit by these worst moments, you will be affected either psychologically, emotionally, or physically.

During these disheartening moments, you are likely to have a mixed reaction depending on your personality. The most common feeling is that of not ready to face others anymore. You may also have a feeling that your dreams have been shattered. You may want to seek revenge. You may desire to take your own life. Or you may want to push on and overcome that moment.

What to Do during Your Worst Moments

Do not make rash decisions during your worst moment. A decision made out of anger will come back to hear you at some point in your life. Take everything slowly. Here are some things I would recommend you do during these moments:

- Despite the effect in your body, make long breaths in and out.

- Even if your body insists on doing something, force yourself to relax.

- Remain in the present moment.

- If you are religious, seek spiritual intervention through prayer.

- Seek medical remedies if possible.

Final Thoughts

After reading this book, you may have realized that life is not a walk in the park. There are sacrifices and adjustments you have to make in an effort to simplify and organize your life, which means that you have to get out of your comfort zone. It is important to understand the meaning of life, what your long-term and short-term goals are, who your role model is, and above all, what stage of life you are in. You should realize that all these efforts are expected to contribute to making your life better and happy.

Living a happy and satisfied life means that you will live a stress-free life. Stress can destroy your life and the lives of those around you. In addition, working under high stress levels leads to underachievement. There are many ways of managing stress levels. First, seek help from close friends or relatives. If that is not comfortable for you, seek professional assistance on ways of managing stress levels in life. It is said that sharing a problem is half solving it. Be careful with people you share your problem with. Some people will take advantage of your situation.

In an effort to organize and simplify your life, time is an important factor. Nobody can ever turn back time. Time that is wasted can never be recovered. The most important thing is to utilize this commodity well. Simple things like making a timetable, timelines, alarms, or reminders are important. You are not a machine; you are prone to forgetting or neglecting things. Nobody is perfect on timekeeping. These reminders will instill discipline into you. Your body is flexible; it takes whatever you teach it. If you create a routine of waking up at 4:00 a.m. every day, you will wake up at that time even without an alarm.

Having read this book, you may have realized how simplifying your life saves you a lot of money. Perhaps you wonder why the richest people in this world still wake up in the morning, probably earlier than you, to go to work. It is because you can never be satisfied with what you have. Do not spend your money around without a plan. Research studies have shown that 75 percent of those who earn a salary at the end of the month depend on debts. Imagine getting a good salary at the end of the month only to remain with nothing five or ten days later.

Live within your means. Life is not a competition. As much as you want to be as successful as your role model or friend, do work hard to be like them. You can never have someone else's life. Pressure from your family to provide what you are not able to is another factor that leads to people not living within their means. Let your family understand the importance of saving. Have an extra coin at the end of the month. Nurture the culture of saving in your kids from an early age. Imagine where you would be right now if you started saving from an early age of fifteen. Take time to read how the richest people in this world made it. Apart from those who inherited their wealth, most of them started building their empires using their savings.

Family and friends are a key factor in living a happy life. Did you know that you spend more than half of your life with your family? Without a happy family, making it in your career, business, or any other project is a difficult task. The strength of a man or a woman is shown by how well they are able to bring their family together. They say, "Show me your friend, and I will tell you who you are." To live an organized life, you have to choose the people you spend time with wisely. Friends can make or break you; they can discourage you. Bad practices, like taking hard drugs, are introduced by friends. This does not mean that you live a life without friends; they are equally important in your life. Choose your friends wisely.

In life, discipline is an important factor. This virtue cuts across all sectors of our lives—your career, finances, schedules, and all other activities of life. Without discipline, living the life that you desire will be like a dream. It is only you who can control your life. As a kid, I used to believe that my life belonged to my parents. For instance, I would work hard in school to make them happy. When I came of age, I realized that parents are just ladders to ensure you have a good future. No one should keep reminding you about the importance of working hard in order to achieve your dreams.

Put all your efforts on the most important things. Begin by understanding what these things are, then put all your energy there. Many times, you waste your time and energy on things that are not important. If you are not sure of the things that matter in your life, look at the things that make you happy. Put your focus on all those things that motivate you every day to go to work.

Never compromise your integrity in an effort to achieve success. Most people today are looking for shortcuts into making it in life. You want to become an overnight millionaire; hence, you are pushed to bend your morals. Things do not work like that; shortcuts are dangerous. A few people might have made it in life through those paths, but it does not mean that the same will apply for you. A friend of mine is serving a ten-year jail term for drug trafficking. I visit him often in jail, and even though he is apologetic about his acts, he cannot change the situation right now. It is too late. That is how shortcuts can mess up your life.

Another important factor is being real to yourself. Understand your strengths and flaws. Many people fail because they set too much expectation on themselves. It is said that you should aim at the sun to reach the sky. Look here—if you set an expectation but at the back of your mind you are sure of not achieving them, trust me, you will not work as hard as you should. Your goals should be dictated by your abilities, time, and available resources. Imagine a scenario where you set a goal of becoming a billionaire in the next two years while you are struggling to pay small bills in your house. Begin by making your family happy. Build them a nice home, buy a car, etc. These are small goals that are achievable. Go for them before thinking of the huge dreams.

Always keep yourself healthy. Without good health, there is nothing you can do. Remember those moments when you were sick and confined in a hospital, very demoralizing. Diet is the key to staying healthy. Read books on choosing the right diet. Another important factor that will help you stay fit is workout. In this book, I have tried to elaborate on the importance of working out. It is through workouts that your body will resist unnecessary diseases. Lifestyle diseases are increasingly becoming a major factor in our lives. The two most important factors are eating the right food and working out frequently.

Also, be accountable for your life. You are responsible for all the decisions you make in your life. Frequently, you want to blame others for your bad decisions. Yes, they may have misadvised you, but the final decision is left for you. They did not force you to make your decision. The faster you accept to take responsibility for your bad choices, the faster you will move on. Above all, mistakes make you a better person. The best thing to do is to learn from your mistakes.

Hygiene is key! It starts with yourself. Being clean and tidy is a personal decision that will better your life. I am a Christian, and I believe that cleanness is next to godliness.

Stop concentrating on things that were meant to grow in your life. Work for what is good and, above all, what is right. Stop beating yourself up over things you have no control over. Drop them! Do this, and your season of greatness will come your way. The elevation of fear, the unknown, and the anxiety are some of the things that distract your path.

Nevertheless, a huge number of people face difficult times simply because of setting unattainable goals. They get tired of trying. This is the reason that you need a motivation life. What wakes you up every day? Be resilient despite the hardships that you may go through every day.

Thus, you should understand that the roadmap to greatness is with disappointments, bumps, failures, and many other challenges. On this road, lessons are learned and possible adjustments are made. Replace those challenges with the determination and will to succeed. Always find a way of turning your challenges into opportunities. Do the right thing. Do not do things to please other people. Do not let your ambitions affect your happiness or relationships of those around you. Let not your happiness depend on others. Trust me, you will hurt yourself trying to please others.

Do not be too desperate in trying to chase your goals. It is a sign of defeat or weakness. If your consciousness serves you right, then you are doing the right thing. If you feel you are not hitting your timelines despite your hard work, maybe it is time to adjust your goals. Make them attainable to yourself.

In this journey, perseverance is key. You may have to endure mistreatment and dependence on others. It is not yet time to quit. Push harder as you look for alternatives. If it is your only source of income, think about how your family will survive without that job.

The value of a simple life may be different for each one of us. There are a lot of benefits that come with eliminating all except what's essential and using your time doing what matters most. With proper organization of your daily activities, you'll realize that you'll have more time to spend doing what you love and with the people that make you happy.

Achieving simplicity is not a walk in the park; it's a continuous journey dotted with many hurdles. But in the end, the mission should help you identify the most important things to do and those that need to be removed. You will get rid of energy-draining fuddle and other messes surrounding your everyday life. Certainly, you would want a situation where all your clean stuff is in order while all the usual distractions are reduced to their minimum.

Simplifying and organizing your life is powerful in changing your life for the better, and there's no better time to do it than right now. Start today and learn how to enhance your happiness. Take charge of your life and avoid wasting any instance of your valuable time.

Made in the USA
San Bernardino, CA
02 September 2019